MONUMENTS OF MUSIC AND MUSIC LITERATURE
IN
FACSIMILE

Second Series—Music Literature

XXII

A BRIEFE DISCOURSE

Of the true (but neglected) use

of Charact'ring the Degrees

THOMAS RAVENSCROFT

A BRIEFE DISCOURSE

Of the true (but neglected) use

of Charact'ring the Degrees

A Facsimile of the London, 1614 Edition

BROUDE BROTHERS LIMITED
NEW YORK

ISBN 0-8450-2222-9

Printed in U.S.A., 1976

NOTE

In Thomas Ravenscroft's *A Briefe Discourse Of the true (but neglected) use of Charact'ring the Degrees* (London, 1614), Page E^r, the Medius-Basis page of No. 12, "Of Drinking Ale and Tobacco," is misnumbered 13, while Pages G^v and G2^r, the second opening of No. 19, "Their Goncluzion," are misnumbered 17. These errors in numeration do not affect the continuity of the text.

A BRIEFE
DISCOVRSE

Of the true (but neglected) vse of Charact'ring *the Degrees by their* Perfection, Imperfection, *and* Diminution
in Measurable Musicke, *against the* Common
Practise *and* Custome *of these*
Times.

Examples *whereof are* exprest *in the*
Harmony *of* 4. Voyces, *Concerning the*
Pleasure *of* 5. *vsuall*
Recreations.

1 *Hunting,* } { 3 *Dauncing*
2 *Hawking,* } { 4 *Drinking,*
5 *Enamouring.*

By Thomas Rauenscroft, *Bachelor*
of Musicke.

LONDON
Printed by Edw: Allde *for* Tho. Adams
1614.

Cum priuilegio Regali.

To the Right Worfhipfull, moſt worthy *Graue* Senators, Guardians, *of* Greſham Colledge *in London.*

Sʳ. *Stephen Soames.*
Sʳ. *Iohn Garret.*
Sʳ. *Thomas Lowe.* } Aldermen
Sʳ. *William Crauen.*

Mʳ. *Cornelius Fiſh.* Chamberlaine

Sᵗ. *Tho: Bennet*
Mʳ. *Tho: Ben-*
net Sheriffe. } Aldermen
Sʳ. *Baptiſt Hicks*
Mʳ. *William Quarles*
Mʳ. *Edward Barnes*
Mʳ. *Iohn Gardiner*
Mʳ. *William Ferrers*
And the 2. *Wardens*

} Of the Mercers Company.

And to the Right Worſhipfull Sir *Iohn Swinerton* and Sir *Thomas Hayes* Knights and Aldermen, moſt True and honourable affectors of *Muſicke.*

S I doe account it a great portion of happines to haue receiu'd firſt *Inſtructions, Exerciſe,* and *Encouragement* of my *Studies* in this *Auncient* and moſt *Famous City:* So am I thereby bound, and doe (willingly) endeuour my beſt part and power, both to teſtifie and augment the *Life* and *Honour* of this *Liberall Science* which I

¶ 2   profeſſe

proʿeſſe, to the benefit of all *Students* therein, and
the contentment of all *Affectors* thereof in this
my natiue *Country*, and eſpecially in this the *Metro-
polis* thereof, which gaue firſt life and breathing to
my poore *Endeauours*. And herein I muſt, and doe
acknowledge it as a ſingular helpe and benefit, that
I haue receiu'd diuers *Inſtructions*, *Reſolutions*, and
Confirmations of ſundry *Points*, and *Præcepts* in our
Art, from the *Muſicke Readers* of that moſt famous
Colledge, founded and erected by the euer praiſe-
worthie, and iuſtly renown'd *Senator* Sr. *Thomas
Creſham*; who bearing his neuer dying Name, as a
Præſident and *Patterne* to his *Co Citizens*, to ſhew
them the right way to æternize their names to fu-
ture poſteritie, by being kinde *Nurſing Fathers* to
good *Literature*, Reuiued the liberall *Arts* and *Scien-
ces*, eſpecially the *Mathematickes*, which were ſomewhat neglected euen in the *Vniuerſities*; and en-
dowed them with ſuch Maintenance and exhibi-
tion, that (their worldly wants being more then
meanly ſupply'd) they haue and doe continually
ſtriue with higheſt *Art* and *Induſtry*, ſo to explaine
them to the world by way of *Lecture*, and otherwiſe, that much good from thence redoundeth to
many deſirous of thoſe *Knowledges*, and more
and more will, as time and occaſion ſhall ſerue.
What fruits my ſelfe in particular haue receiu'd
by

by that one particular *Lecture* of *Musicke* (whereof I was an vnworthie *Auditor*) I dutifully
acknowledge to haue proceeded from that *Colledge*;and doe heere *Commende* and *Dedicate* them
to your *Worshipps*, Who are *Visitors* and *Guardians*
of that most famous *Foundation*, from whence I
haue receiu'd such benefit in these my studies. For
as I haue beene encouraged by your Noblenes to
trauaile in these Studies,so by Dutie they belong to
You, from whome they had their *Animation*. May
it therefore please your *Worships* to accept this my
Discourse of *Musicke* with some *Harmonicall Examples* thereof,as a *Simple Sacrifice*, in part of that
deuotion and seruice which I owe, vpon promise
and full intendment by your wonted goodnes
and asistance, to search for Richer and riper *Disco-
ueries* in this *Musicall Continent*. So wishing the
long Continuance of your carefull *Loue*,and lo-
uing *Care* to al good *Learning*, especially to *Musicke*,
the earthly *Solace* of Mans *Soule*, I euer Remaine

The *Honourer*, and sincere *Affector*

of your Approued

good Mindes

Thomas Rauenscroft.

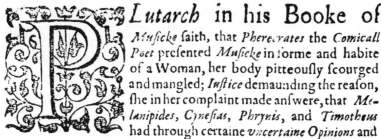

Lutarch in his Booke of *Muficke* faith, that *Pherecrates* the *Comicall Poet* prefented *Muficke* in forme and habite of a Woman, her body pitteoufly fcourged and mangled; *Iuftice* demaunding the reafon, fhe in her complaint made anfwere, that *Melanipides, Cynefias, Phrynis,* and *Timotheus* had through certaine *vncertaine Opinions* and *Changes*, wrought her fo much woe.

If *Pherecrates* had now liued, well and truely might he haue haue prefented her * *Pannis annisᵹ obfitam,* with fcarce *Ligatures* left to ⁎ *Terent.* preferue the compacture of her *Body*, fo much is fhe wrong'd, dilacerated, difmembred, and difioynted in thefe our daies; fhe fcarcely hath *Forme* or *Habite* left, but e'ne as a *Sceleton*, retaines onely a fhape, or fhadowe, of what fhe was in her former purity.

Now may fhe fit complayning, O woe is me, that was ordain'd for the welfare of all vertue in *Man*; O woe is me, that to whome I brought fo much goodneffe, by him I fhould be vilified, and fo ill intreated; O woe is me, that for whome, and for whofe beft good I ordain'd *Lawes* and *Precepts*, by him, and onely him, I fhould be thus abuf'd, my *Lawes* violated, my *Precepts* reiected, and my felfe made a laughing ftocke; O woe is me, that e're I was, or did fo much good for *him* that fets fo light by *me*.

And (if euer) this braine-ficke *Age* wherein we liue, may beft teftifie her mifery; for neither *Her felfe*, nor her *Lawes* are regarded euen of her *Children*, but moft led by their ftragling paffions runne after their owne rebellious Imaginations; which doth breed a mifery of miferies vnto *Her*, great griefe and forrow to her true borne *Children*, and to all, a bafe wretched *Eftimation*, afwell amongft thofe who know her *Eminencie*, as thofe who neuer knew *Her*, nor any other vertue.

And if we fhall finde (as certainely finde we fhall) in one member of *Her*, in one little part of her *Precepts*, fo many erroneous and repugnant *Abfurdities* committed, what fhould we meete with, if we did fearch into her whole *Body* ? furely fuch a contumelious *Infurrection*, that either for Ignorance or fhame in fo much wronging *Her*, we muft ftand obftinate, and fet *Her* at defiance, or with peaceable vnderftanding fubmit our felues to *Her Cenfure*, checking our

wilfull

wilfull Nature, correcting our Ignorance, reforming all offences, with submiſſiue obedience to follow the *Lawes* and *Præcepts* by *Her* ordain'd, whereby we ſhall returne into grace and fauour with *Her*, and be graced and fauoured of all *Hers*; for ſhe commendeth her *Founders* and *Fauourers*, and ſhe honoureth all thoſe who entertaine *Her*.

And now in the behalfe of my *Mother Muſicke*, as a dutiful childe to condole, and (to my power) ro miniſter a Medicine to *Her* Maladies, haue I oppoſ'd my ſelfe againſt a Capitall Rebell *Common Practiſe*, or *Cuſtome*, which long ſince ſeditiouſly reſiſted, & through arrogancy and jgnorance hath incenſt againſt *Her*, and drawne away the moſt part of her *Children* from their due allegeance; whereby I entend either to right *Her*, by reclaiming them to the *Line* of her *Lawes* and *Præcepts*, or to make knowne vnto the world all her *Spurious* and Illegitimate *Children*, that doe thus vnnaturally oppoſe themſelues againſt *Her*.

For Iudges whereof on *Muſickes* behalfe, I haue choſen moſt worthy and Iuditious *Senators* of *Her* Common-wealth, who following her *Præcepts* and *Lawes* from their Infancy, haue ſought (as their *Enſamples* teſtiſie) to the vt'moſt of their powers, to reduce all to *Her* gouernment.

For Iudges on their ſide, although I could nominate many, and thoſe *Capitall Maiſters* too (for ſo they are accounted of the *Rebellious Rowte*, whom in regard of ignorant eſtimation of their worth, or worthleſſe eſtimation, I forbeare to name;) yet may they be knowne to all, becauſe they will be the firſt that will *oppoſe*, & the iaſt and leaſt that will, or can alleadge *Reaſon* for their *Tenents*; only they will vrge effæminately their owne *Will*, or paſſionately their owne *Fancy*, or that they haue ſeene the contrary, and their *Enſamples* in *Print*; but true Iudgement will be able to conuince ſuch *Humoriſts*, and to ſift out the *flowre of Truth* from the *huskes of Error* in this Muſicall *Monomachie*. For as it is ſufficient commendations for an honeſt *Cato*, if he be diſparaged in his reputation but by ſome diſſolute, diſordered *Clodius*, or *Cataline*: ſo can there be no greater approbation of any *Facultie*, or *Science* whatſoeuer, then to be oppung'd and diſcommended by an *Ignorant Artiſt*, or ſome *rawe Profeſſor* of the ſame *Myſteries*.

And ſuch be they (if there be any, as I doubt too many) for the moſt part, whome *Horace* termes *Humorous Singſters*, ſuch as
Arcabius

Arcadius was, saying of such,

(1) *Vt nunquam inducant animum cantare, rogati,*
  Iniussi nunquam desistant:

(1) *Horat. Sa-tyr. 3.lib. I.*

Thus Englished by *Doctor Case*, a *Mecenas* of *Musicke*,

(2) Praise of *Mus* to the Reader.

(2) *That being prai'd to sing and shew their skill,*
  Cannot induced be, say what thou list :
  But vnrequested keepe a chaunting still,
  And from their folly neuer will desist.

(3) *Glareanus* termes them *Common Cantors* or *Chaunters*, of whom
(4) *Plutarch* (according to the Prouerbiall verse) saith,

(3) *Glareanus Dodecachordi.* lib. 3. cap. 8. *Ibidem* lib. 3. cap 9.
(4) *Plutarch Simposiackes* lib. I.

A Begger can no Begger well abide,
  And Chaunters one by th'other *is enuy'de :*

And by diuers others they are term'd *Custcmable Composers* ; But
(5 *Ornithoparckus* saith, they entitle themselues the *Musitians* of
Musitians, per excellentiam, who being ignorant of all things in our
Art, yet brag of their *generall Knowledge*; & one discouering such
Natures saith,

(5) *Ornitho-parchus* lib. 2. cap. 8.

Such doe contend without the cause discerning,
  And argue most of that they haue no learning.

But let their owne fancies and arrogancies either Confirme, or
Confute them; for by their meanes, (and onely them) is grounded
in the heart of *Greatnes,* that our *Arts Greatnes* is great onely in a
Base, whereby she is fallen to such *Vilitie,* that the *Learned* are
weary thereof, the *Ignorant* ashamed, *Themselues* despis'd, made a
mockery, and a Iesting stocke, onely seruing (and good) for no
other vse, then to satisfie their Barbarous affections, which are like
those of the(6) *Polititian Archidamus,* (or such like *Secretaries*) whose
Belly was his Idoll, made more account of a *Caterer,* then a *Cantor.*

(6) Praise of *Musi* fol. 27.

But the more the pitty, too too many such *Polititians* there are
in these dayes, who esteeme of *Musicks Professors* no otherwise
(nay scarce so much) then they doe of *Hunters* and *Faulkoners,* and
to deserue (at the most) no better to be rewarded, or regarded.
These are no better then *Monstra Hominum:* with *Lucinus* the

¶ ¶   *Emperour*

Emperour they esteeme *Learning* and all *Vertue* to be the *Bare* and *plague* of a Common-wealth : And yet (forsooth) these *Archidamuses* will seeme to countenance and entertaine *Musicks Professors;* But alas it is vpon *Colour* and *Praetext*, to make shew vnto the world that there is in them a *Musicall Genius*, and a religious disposition; they make this their vertue, to shadow such inhumane desires, for the better accomplishing of their priuate ends. And when their humours are to be besotted with the *Soule-rauishing* pleasure and content of melodious *Harmony*, they seeke either by dissembling *Commendations*, or grosse *Flattery*, or the like, (by any ordinary capacity quickly conceiued)to grieue and discontent those *outwardly*, who affoord them delight,and contentment *inwardly*.

What pollicies are vs'd in the *Entertaining* of these *Professors*, in the *Retaining* of them, and in their small *Salaries* and *Pittances* (which they terme *Competencies*) I forbeare at this time to disclose; But let such *Golden Sheepe*, who are better *Clad* then *Taught*,& wanting an ingenuous & generous disposition,are willing to prostitute themselues to *Daunce* after euery mans *Pipe*, or to *Fiddle* at euery mans*Whistle*,be as they deserue;I could wish & aduice al *Students* of our *Art*, or any other noble *Science* and *Speculatiue Facultie* whatsoeuer, to account of *Such* as they account of *Them*, and to stand firme for the honour and estimation of *Learning*.

But to our former discourse: Most men respect *Parasites* most, who soothingly feede,and flatter them in their naturall affections, but reiect and despise those *Tell-troths* who discouer their follies. Let *Common Practise* and her *Complices* censure me as they please, building vpon a good foundation I am prepar'd; For 'tis neither *Vaine-glory*,nor *Ambition* that I ayme at, but onely the *Honour* of our *Art*, to vindicate *Her* from these *Solæcismes*,and *Barbarismes*, wherewith she is now pestred. I loue and reuerence the vnderstanding *Artist* and naturall *Affector*, as life; but detest the selfe-conceited pertinacious *Arrist*,and politick *Fauourite* as death;& both shall be knowne by their affecting,or censuring of me.

It is an *easie matter* (saith one) to finde *fault*; & an *ordinary matter*(say I) tis to commit a *fault*, and there is no reason but *faults* (especially great ones as these are) should be corrected.

(1) *Franchinus* obserued these errors in the *Common Practise*, and reiected them.

(1) *Gla: Dod:*
lib. 3 cap 8.

Glareanus

(²) *Glareanus* likewise fought to reforme them.

(³) *Morley* acknowledged them for errors; but was loath to break the *Common Practife*, or receiued *Cuftome*; yet if any would change, he would be the firft that fhould follow.

(²) *Glar: Dodi:* lib 3.cap.I I. (³) *Morley Annota: an Tripla-proportion.*

The Ice is broken, and the Foot-path found; and I hope to finde many *Morleyes* aliue, though *He* (who did fhine as the *Sunne* in the *Firmament* of our *Art*, and did firft giue light to our vnderftanding with his *Præcepts*) be long fince come to the *Clofe* and *Period* of his *Time*; But his pofterity, as *Starres*, receiuing light and benefit from his *Labours*, will (I hope) according to his defire and wifhes, entertaine and embrace fuch *Opinions*, as he himfelfe acknowledg'd to be true.

In this little *Treatife* I haue not obferu'd onely the *Writings* of Authors (becaufe I found them various and differing among themfelues; Some obferu'd the cuftome of the *Common Practife* : Others not onely the *Practife*, but the *Reafon* of each particular *Præcept* : A third, well vnderftanding neither *Theory* nor *Practife*, drew out certaine *Rules* from both the former, and according to their owne *Imaginations* deliuer'd *abfurd Opinions*) but I haue fearch't the very *Originall* of our *Art*, and *Etimologie* of each proper *Terme*; how, & wherto each thing is appropriated; I haue compar'd the *Practife* with the *Theory*, *Nature* with our *Art*, and *it* with other *Arts*, and I finde it a Subordinate *Mathematicke*, extracted from the Quinteffence of *Arithmetick* in the *Rules* and *Præcepts*.

So that then (Courteous Reader) if thou find'ft *Reafon* and *Authority* for my *Affertions*, neither mifconftrue me, nor condemne me without better *Reafon*, *Proofe*, and *Authority*, then heere I alleadge; And although diuers may produce *Authors* (and happily the felfe fame which I alleadge) yet fhal they finde that thofe *Authors* themfelues acknowledge to haue receiu'd them from the *Common Practife*, and not from the *Fundamentall Reafons* of the *Grounds* and *Rules* of our *Art*; But till then, if thou accept and entertaine them, my defires and labours haue their accomplifh'd & wifh'd for, rewards.

If any obiect, that thofe former *Harmonies* by mee publifhed in my *Infancy* are contrary to thefe my obiections ; I anfwere, I did then as a *Childe* ; I did follow *Enfamples* more then *Reafons* ; and thofe Workes for the moft part were not Compos'd by *My felfe*, but by diuers and fundry *Authors*, which I neuer the leffe compil'd together, in regard of the generall delight men tooke in them;

¶ ¶ 2 And

And although very many of them were *Defectiue* in their Comp_sition when they came to my hands : yet according to my know-ledge then, I *corrected* them and *commended* them to the world, and had the *Printer* and *Presse-Corrector* discharg'd their office with care, they had appear'd without any defect in their *Cliffes*, *Notes*, and *Ditties*, though most part of their *Measures* in the *Prolation* and *Di-minutions* (following the *Commom Practise*) are falsely *Character'd;* the which, by this fourth and last worke of *Ionick Harmonies*, may be corrected.

The *Forraine Artist* saith, that an *Englishman* is an excellent *Imi-tator*, but a very bad *Inuentor*; and indeed it should so appeare; for we obseruing such *Inuentions* which they ensample to vs, as *Madri-galls*, *Pastorals*, *Neapolitanes*, *Ballads*, and diuers other light *Har-monies*, doe bend our courses onely to surpasse the *tuning* of such *Strings*; Among whome if diuers excellent *Composers* haue excee-ded their *Ensamples*, why should not we (seeing our *Art* is as copi-ous and ample, our *Clymate* not exceeding moist, and our *Artists* (as they confesse) farre surpasse them in the accuratenes thereof, which is vpon the *Plaine song*, and *multiplicity of Parts*, wherein they doe admire vs,) finde some *Inuention* to set them on worke? Surely the fault is in our slothfull *Natures*, either not aiming at the foresaid *Perfection*, or not making *Vse* of those knowledges for *Inuention*, which they would direct vs vnto.

Wherefore let vs for the honour of our *Art*, of our *Selues* and *Countrye*, (especially those whome she maintaines) endeauour to bring *Her* vnto that *Life*, *Reputation*, *Estimation* and honour, which she formerly did sustaine; so shall wee acknowledge our selues her *True-borne Children*, and knowe *Her selfe* to be a vertuous *Mother* and *Nurse*, ar d the *World* will esteeme *Her* according to her *Desire*, and reward vs according to our *Deserts*, and all receiue *Comfort* and *Contentment*, according to that power, which she affoordeth.

In Approbation of this Worke.

IN former Age, among Muſitians rare,
  Regard was had of Meaſures then in vſe
And Characters ; ordain'd by ſpeciall care,
  Leaſt after-Cōmers ſhould the ſame abuſe;
But foraſmuch as thoſe Compoſers Sage
Occaſion had not to apply each thing
Vnto the diuers Humours which this Age
  Hath ſtudied out, and to the world doth bring :
I well approue this Authors Diligence,
  Who by his Labour Characters hath found,
To ſhew what heretofore by neglig nce
  Hath beene omitted, and for certaine ground
To make that plaine, that wanting was before
  In Meaſures, Times, Prolations well obſeru'd.
Wherein his Commendations is the more,
  His Songs, and Skill high Praiſe hath well deſeru'd.

NATHANIELL GYLES Bachelar of Muſicke,
  Maiſter of the Children of his Maieſties
  Chappels, of Houſehold, and Windſor.

Of this Enſuing Diſcourſe.

MArkes that did limit Lands in former times
  None durſt remoue; ſo much the common good
Preuail'd with all men; 'twas the worſt of crimes.
  The like in Muſicke may be vnderſtood,
For That the treaſure of the Soule is, next
  To the rich Store-houſe of Diuinity :
Both comfort Soules that are with care perplext,
  and ſet the Spirit Both from paſſions free.

¶¶ 3   The

The Markes that limit Muſicke heere are taught,
  So fixt of ould, which none by right can change,
Though Vſe much alteration hath wrought,
  To Muſickes Fathers that would now ſeeme ſtrange.
The beſt embrace, which herein you may finde,
  And th'Author praiſe for his good Worke, *and* Minde.

THO: CAMPION.

IOHN DOWLAND *Bachelar* of *Muſicke*, and *Lu-tenist* to the *Kings* Sacred *Maieſtie*, in com-mendation of this *Worke.*

F Igurate Muſicke *doth in each* Degree
  Require it Notes, *of ſeuerall* Quantity ;
By Perfect, *or* Imperfect Meaſure *chang'd :*
And that of More, *or* Leſſe, *whoſe* Markes *were rang'd*
By Number, Circle, *and* Poynt: *but various vſe*
Of vnskild Compoſers *did induce*
Confuſion, *which made muddy and obſcure,*
What firſt Inuention *fram'd moſt cleere, and pure.*
Theſe, (worthy RAVENSCROFT) *are reſtrain'd by* Thee
To one fixt Forme : *and that approu'd by* Me.

In *the moſt iuſt praiſe of* Muſicke, *this praiſe-worthy* Worke, *and my deare, vertu-ous, and right expert friend,*
the moſt iudicious
Author.

T He *ten-fold* Orbes *of* Heauen *are ſaid to moue*
  By Muſicke; *for, they make* Harmonious *din :*
And all the Powres ſubordinate *aboue*
  Spend Time, *nay, ſpend* Æternity *therein.*

If

If Muficke *then, moue all that* All doth moue;
    That's not compriz'd in A L L *that fpights her State :*
If not in A L L, *it's nought; which who doth loue*
    is worfe then nought, to loue what Heau'n doth hate :
For, N O V G H T *is nothing; fith it was not made*
    By that great W O R D, *without which made was nought :*
Then, if that nought but N O V G H T *doe her inuade,*
    Like God, her goodneffe is furmounting T H O V G H T?
But no man is fo ill that hath no good;
    So, no man in the Abftract *can be nought :*
Then 'tis no man that hates fweete Muficke moode,
    But Some-thing worfe then all that can be thought.
A Beaft *? O no :* A Monfter *? neither. Then*
    Is it a Deuill *? Nothing leffe : for, thefe*
Haue Beings *with an* Angell, or a Man;
    But that exifts not, that fweete Notes difpleafe.
F O R M E S, Effence *giue to* Man, Beaft, Fifh, *&* Fowle;
    Then Men WERE *not, had they no* Soule *(their* Forme)
But Muficke *haters haue no* Forme, *nor* Soule :
    So, they (like Sinne *) exift but to enorme,*
For, had they Soules *produc'd in* Harmony,
    Or rather Are it felfe *(fome* Wife auouch *)*
They would be rauifht with her Suauity,
    And turn'd Cœleftiall *with her* Heauenly Touch *!*
But, let them goe as more than mortall Sinne
    Gainft Wifedomes Spirit, *not to be forgiuen :*
While thou doft wooe the Soules, *which thou doft winne*
    With thy fweet Notes *(deere* Friend *)to* mind but Heau'n.
Thy Nature, Manners, *and thy* Notes *doe make*
    A Three-fold-Cord, *to drawe all hearts it gaines :*
Thy Muficke Cordes *hold* Eares *and* Eyes *awake*
    (Yet lullaby in pleafure) with their Straines.
So, then this latter Muficke *(though alone)*
    'Twixt Fame *and* Thee *doth make an* Vnifon,
    Through which confent, though Deaths *clouds thee o'rerun*
Thy glory ftill fhall fhine, and cloud the Sun.

                    Io: Dauies. Heref:

                                        In

In Approbation of this ensuing Discourse, and the Author therof my deare friend, Maister Thomas Ravenscroft.

ARts are much alt'red from their Pristine State,
Humors and Fancies so predominate.
Ould Artists though they were Plaine, yet were Sure,
Their Præcepts and their Principles were Pure:
But now a dayes We scarce retaine the Grounds,
W'are so Extrauagant beyond our Bounds.
Among the Rest, Musicke (that noble Art)
In this sad Elegie must beare a Part;
Whose Purity was such in times of yore,
(When Theory the Practise went before)
That then She was had in as great Esteeme
As now of Her the Vulgar basely Deeme.
Errors in Figures, Characters, and Note
Doe Now cause many Teach, and Learne by rote.
This my deare Friend doth seeke heere to amend;
Wherein he trauail'd farre, great paines did spend
To right his Mother; he seekes to reduce
Her to her auntient Grounds, and former Vse,
To beate downe Common Practise, that doth range
Among the Commons, and her Præcepts change.
Heere shall you finde of Measures diuers sorts,
For Church, for Madrigalls, for sundry Sports;
Heere shall you finde true Iudgement, store of reading,
All for the Ould true Rules of Musicke pleading.
Numbers of 3. among the Meane respected
Are hence exil'd, and (worthily) reiected,
As being crept in by Custome, and Vse
Among the Vulgars, which the Wise refuse.
Much might be said more of this little Booke:
But let the Reader iudge that on't shall looke.

Thi

This of the Author *onely I will say,*
That in One *poynt to no man he giues way:*
Compoſing of *a* Song *vnto ſome* Ditty
He is ſo Iudicious *and ſo* Witty,
That waighing firſt the Nature *of each* Word
He ſindes ſit Notes, *that thereunto accord,*
Making both Sound *and* Sence *well to agree;*
Witneſſe *his ſundry* Songs *of* Harmonie.
What ſhall I ſay more? this Worke *I approoue,*
And for his Skill, *and* Paines *the* Author *loue.*

Bachelar of Muſicke.

To him that reades.

C Oncord *and* Diſcord *ſtill haue beene at ods*
   Since the firſt howre the Heathens *made them* Gods.
In euery Profeſſion, Trade, *or* Art
They draw their ſwords, and each Wit *takes a part.*
There's neither Starre *that moues, nor* Hearbe *that growes,*
But they Diſpute *vpon't with* Words, *or* Blowes.
'Mongſt which Muſitians, *hanging vp their* Harpes
Doe growe to fall Flat out, *for* Flats *and* Sharpes,
And by their Diſcord *make that* Art *vneuen,*
Whoſe Concord *ſhould expreſſe that* Peace *in* Heauen;
But heere is One, *whoſe* Doue-like *Pen of* Peace
Striues to out-flie ſuch Strife, *and make it ceaſe;*
And Diſcord *brings with* Concord *to agree,*
That from their Strife *he raiſes* Harmonie.
He that for Loue *doth* This, *and not for* Gaine,
Muſt needes haue Praiſe, *the proper due for* Paine.

WILLIAM AVSTIN.
¶ ¶ ¶

To my deare Friend Maister
THOMAS RAVENSCROFT,
vpon this *Worke*.

I Prophesie (deare Friend) that thou which giu'st
The Dead deserued Bayes, shalt while thou liu'st
Neuer want Garlands of that SacredTree
To Crowne thee in Æternall memorie :
Thou that hast made the dying Coales to Glowe
Of ould Ed: Piers his name; which now shall growe
('Gainst all that enuious or malicious bee)
In high Opinion 'mongst Posteritie;
Nor shall they touch Worth without Reuerence,
In whome once dwelt such perfect Excellence
In Heaun'ly Musicke ; I may call it so,
If ould Pythagoras said truely, who
Affirm'd that the Sphæres Cælestia'l
Are in their Motion truly Musicall:
And Man, in whome is found a humane Minde,
(Then Whome, (Angells except) who e're could finde
A Nobler Creature) some affirme consisteth
Onely of Harmony, wherein existeth
The Soule of Musicke; and yet (but for Thee)
This Man had dy'd to all mens memorie;
Whose Name (now cleans'd from rust) this Worke of thine
(While there are Times or Men) I doe deuine
Shall keepe Aliue; nor shall thy owne Name die,
But by this Worke liue to Æternitie :
And from it men hereafter shall pull out
Scourges, to lash the base Mechanicke Rout
Of Mercenary Minstrels, who haue made
(To their owne scorne) this Noble Art, a Trade.

THO: PIERS.

In Laudem huius opusculi.

NI bona (prisca licèt) non consuetudo ferenda;
  Dirue, quod rectum ius negat esse suum.
Sit speciosa licèt tua, si sit adultera forma,
  Vera magis grata est, altera fucus erit.
Iste *Notas* pariterq; *Nothas* dat (perlege *Lector*)
  Quêis miserè est rudibus *Musica* læsa *Liber*,
Est dignus quem sæpe legas facilisq; paratu est:
  Multus in *Authorem* sit tuus ergo fauor.

T. H.

De ingenuo Iuvene T. R. *(annos* **22.** *nato)* *Musicæ*
Studiosissimo, huius Libelluli
Authore.

RAra auis *Arte Senex* Iuvenis; Sed rarior est, si
  Aetate est juvenis, *Moribus* ille Senex.
Rara auis est *Author*; (pœné est pars (1) *Nominis* vna)   (1) *Rauens-*
  Namq; annis juvenis, *Moribus, Arte* Senex.   *croft.*
(2) Non vidit tria Lustra *Puer*, quin *Arte* probatus,   (2) *Ad annos*
  Vitâ laudatus, Sumpsit in *Arte* Gradum.   *14. Creatus est*
Quale fuit studium, *Liber* hic testabitur; in quo   *Baccalaureus*
  Vim, Vitam Numeris reddidit ille *Nouam.*   *facultatis Mu-*
Quám bené castigat, malé quos induxerat *Vsus*   *sica in acâdem:*
  Errores, *Priscas* hîc renouando *Notas?*   *Cantabrig.*
  Arte Senex, *Virtute* Senex, *ætate* Adolescens
  I bone, *Rara auis es*; Scribe *bonis auibus.*

R. LL. Theo-muso-philus.

FINIS.

THE

THE PREFACE.

Vſicke in ancient times, was held in as great *Eſtimation*, *Reue-rence*, and *Honour*, by the *Beſt vnderſtandings* and *Nobleſt Bloods*, as any *Sci-ence Liberall* whatſoeuer. The *Graue Philoſophers* re-puted it an *Inuention* of the *Gods*, which they had beſtowed on *Men*, to make them *better conditi-oned*, then bare *Nature* affoorded : And the *Wiſe Grecians* therefore educated their children in *it*, that by meanes of *it*, they might *temper* their mindes, and fully ſettle therein, the *Vertues of Modeſtie and Honeſty* : and, (in a word) *all of worth* euer held it, a very *Direct* and *Neceſſary* courſe, for the beſt *Inſtitution of Life*, and *Correction of ill manners*.

The *Cauſes* then of that *Diſrepute, and ouer lowe Eſtimation*, which *Muſicke* in theſe dayes, (for the moſt part) ſuſtaines, and whether they proceed from *Corruptions of Nature*, or *Art*, or both, as long ſince I began to meruaile at, ſo had I now vttered ſome obſeruations thereabout, had not counſaile, and diſcretion perſwaded me a while for a fur-ther exact ſuruay.

I had then (amidſt other things) vnfolded on the one ſide, both the *Naturall*, and alſo the *Politick Affector* and

A · · · · · · · · · · · · · · · · · · · *Entertayner*

Entertayner of our *Art*, and on the other side, the strange *imbecillity of our Professors*, a great part of them *Profest Generall Maisters*, able (they will vndertake) fully to teach both *precepts* and *Practise* of our *Art*, in one poore yeare, (or lesse if you will:) and yet (spoken it shall be without offence) the most of them, not well vnderstanding the very *Nature* of a *Sound*, or the *Difference* of *Properties*, the *Distinction* of *Tones*, the *Dinision* of *Numbers and Measures*, the *inæqualitie* of *Proportions*, nay, scarse Defining the nature of that *Instrument*, Maisters whereof they professe themselues to be.

I had likewise poynted at some other abuses, committed and suffered by *Musicks Professors*, as well in *Ecclesiasticke* as *Common Seruice*, whereby the one, findes his Due Right empayred; & the other, his Estimation; and both, their Abilities.

As for those common kinde *Practitioners*, (truly ycleped *Minstrells*, though our City makes *Musitians* of them) who making account forsooth to doe the *Art* Honour, now in these daies of the ill opinion, and small credit it beares, haue (fairely) brought it downe from a cheife *Liberall Science*, to the basest almost of *Mechanick Functions*: I make no question, but in good time it may returne vpon their owne necks, and their Desert be rewarded, as Statute in that case hath already (most worthily) prouided.

Besides, I suppose I should hardly haue omitted the Beleefe (whereof I finde some *Aery* or *Instrumentall Composers* and *Practitioners* to be) concerning certaine Vices, which their Ignorance is perswaded, our *Art* receiues helpe by, how disagreeing soeuer, both to *Nature* and *Reason*, which is the soule of all *Arts*.

And then for amends of all, I should at last, haue affoorded somewhat in the generall precepts, both of *Plaine*, and *Measurable Musick*, in the many *Diuersities*, which the *Nature* of *Compositions* giue vs, from the very *originall* of them, to

that

that *excellencie*, wherein the *Art* is now to be found, and in divers other particulars tending to the same effect.

But now in the meane time, let the *Affecter* shew his *Disposition*, and the *Professor* his *Art*, to both whome I promife, that when e're I proceed in it, I will be free and impartiall, as Rule and Reafon onely giues me, laying my Obferuations, and fo defiring (if it may be) the reftitution of our Science, to Due, and ancient Honour.

And till then (if at all they loue the *Art*) they shall well accept of my good will, and (with me) take in good worth, thefe *various Sprightfull, Delightfull Harmonies,* which now I bring them. Their *Compofure* I dare warrant, 'tis not onely of *Ayre,* made for fome fmall tickling of the outward Sence alone, but a great deale more folide, and fweetly vnited to *Number, Meafures,* and *Nature* of the *Ditty.* The earneft affections which a man hath, in the vfe of fuch *Recreations* as they are made for, are fo fully expreft in them, for *Tact, Prolation,* and *Diminution,* that not onely the *Ignorant* Eare muft needs be pleafed with them, for their *Variety* of *fweet Straynes,* and the *Humorous Fantaftick* eare fatiffied, in the *Iocundity* of their many *Changes,* but alfo the *Iudicious* hearer will finde that in them, which paffes the *Outward* fence, & ftrikes a *rare delight of Paffion* vpon the *Mind* it felfe, that attends them.

I will take fo much *Iudgement* vpon me, as to affirme, I finde a *great* part of them fo, though (without any tryall) the very *Naming* of thofe *two Worthies* in their *Art, and Times,* (and efpecially in thefe *kinds*) who firft *Compofed* that part I now fpeake of, is warrant inough for fuch a Beleefe of them Maifter *Edward Pearce* the firft, fometimes Maifter of the Children of Saint *Paules* in London, and there my Maifter, a man of fingular eminency in *his Profeffion,* both in the *Educating* of *Children* for the ordering of the *Voyce* fo, as the *Quality* might afterward *credit* him and *preferre*

ferre them : And alſo in thoſe his *Compoſitions* to the
Lute, whereof, the world enioyes many, (a s from the
Maiſter of that Inſtrument) together with his skilfull Inſtructions for other Inſtruments too, as his fruits can beare
him witneſſe.

The ſecond I name, as partner in this worke, is Maiſter
Iohn Bennet, a Gentleman admirable for all kindes of *Com-*
poſures, either *in Art, or Ayre, Simple or Mixt,* of what
Nature ſoeuer. I can eaſily beleeue he had ſomwhat more
then *Art,* euen ſome *Naturall inſtinct* or *Better Inſpiration,* by
which, in all his workes, the very *life* of that *Paſſion,*
which the *Ditty* ſounded, is ſo truely expreſt, as if he had
meaſured it alone by his owne Soule, and inuented no o-
ther *Harmony,* then his owne ſenſible feeling in that *Affecti-*
on did affoord him.

As for this little worke, and the Diuerſities therein,
they appertayne all, to the common *Recreations* that men
take, and therein vtter that Paſſion which men diſcouer in
the vſe of thoſe *Recreations* :   As are

$$\left\{\begin{array}{l}\textit{1 Hunting}\\\textit{2 Hawking}\end{array}\right\}\qquad\left\{\begin{array}{l}\textit{3 Dauncing}\\\textit{4 Drinking}\end{array}\right\}$$

$$\textit{5 Enamoring :}$$

All which are here as liuely Characteriz'd, as euer were
any of the kind yet among vs, withall *Meaſure,* and *Rule*
to *Art* appertayning.

1. 2.

Hunting & *Hawking* haue the firſt place, as the moſt *gene-*
rous and *worthy* kindes of *Recreations.* In the *performance*
of both which, ſuch are the *Times, Numbers,* and *Meaſures,*
obſeruable, not in *Man* alone that vſes the *Paſtime,* but euen
in the *Creatures* alſo, that either *make* the *Game,* or *purſue* it,

S

as being duely *Composed*, beget an *excellent Harmony*, and require the *Singers skill* to vtter them, as if he were then abroad at the *performing* of them.

3.

THe next we present is *Dauncing*, but that with some difference from the common *Exercise* now a daies of it, in our *Maskes* and *Reuells*: As not grounded on the *Dauncing* of *Measures*, and accordingly bound to some particular *Rules* and *Numbers*, proper to the *Nature* of that *Daunce* one-ly, which then is afoot : But fashioned like those *Antique Daunces*, which the *Poets* would haue vs beleeue, the *Fayries*, and the *Satyres*, and those other *Rurall Natures* frequented, and hauing in them, much more *variety* and *change* then any other *Composition*, and withall so expressing our *imperfect Moods* and *Measures*, for their *Tact*, *Prolation*, and *Diminution*, that in singing, *cunningly* and *Sprightfully* to resemble them, must needs giue the *performance* high commendation, and the Hearer the most pleasing delight that may be.

4.

DRinking is our *fourth Recreation*. For so 'tis become (at least, if not the *first*) by the *vse* & *Delight* that men now take in it, and so, for their sakes, I am content now to terme it. And among all the rest, for theirs Especially, that in the *Aery* part of our *Faculty*, for want of *Skill* and *Reason* in that which they *performe*, set their *Strength and Spirits* to search it out of the other *Elements*, chiefly out of those two, that the *Ayre* is euuironed with, *Fire and Water*, well *compos'd and Brew'd* together, wherein they are resolued to grow *exceeding skilfull*, or else it shal cost their Braines a fiering, and their Bowells a drowning. The *Earth* indeed they looke least after, t'is base that they account, and for Mechanick Spirits to runne so lowe, The *Note* they sing

A 3   is is of a higher *Strayne*, their *Recreation* lies in a brauer *Element*, wherein they *houer*, so *vnlike Men*, so long, so *desperatly*, that at last, in their *miserable ends*, they scarce get the *Earth* honestly to couer them.

'Tis not then either for *Direction* or *Incouragement* herein, that I would be thought to bring this *part*; they that take me so, much mistake me, who can better hope, that the perfect *presentation* of this illaudable *demeanour*, will turne this *Sport* into so much *Earnest*, as shall teach the *Innocent Auditor* to *loath* them, if perhaps not *reclayme* the *guilty*.

5.

OVr last *Recreation* heere, is, that they terme *Enamoring*, a *Passion* as (more or lesse) possessing and affecting all, so truely exprest by none, but *Musick*, that is, *Song*, or *Poetry* : the former whereof, giues herein both a *relish*, and a *beauty* to the latter, inasmuch as *Passionate Tunes* make *Amorous Poems* both willinglier heard, and better remembred. I haue heard it said, that *Loue* teaches a man *Musick*, who ne're before knew what pertayned thereto: And the Philosophers three *Principall Causes* of *Musick*, 1. *Dolour*, 2. *Ioy*, 3. *Enthusiasme* or *rauishing of the Spirit*, are all found by him within *Loues* Territories. Besides, we see the *Soueraignty* of *Musicke* in this *Affection*, by the *Cure* and *Remedy* it affoords the *Dispassionate*, and *Infortunate Sonnes of Loue*, thereby to asswage the *turmoyles*, and quiet the *tempests* that were raised in them.

ANd here now, 'twere high time for me to make an end of *Prefacing*, did I not foresee, that the different *Character* which herein I giue the *Time* of these *Compositions*, may perhaps seeme strange to the *Performer*, because, how'ere the *Tact*, according to the seuerall *Motions*, is vulgarly knowne, yet is it altogether *vn-art-like Chatactered*, *ractered*, and accordingly the *Practife* of them, (amongft vs efpecially) not aright expreft. To approue them therefore to the *Mufes*, and to warrant them, for the true *Forme* of *Charactering* the *Time*, both in *imperfect* and *perfect Meafures*: As alfo to preuent the *Ignorant*, that they venture not, (without better *Reafon* of the *Art*, then I fhall giue them) præiudicioufly to draw the common *Practife* for an *Argument* againft me, I will now, in as few words as well I may, præmife fome particular *Notions and Rules* in the *Meafurable part of Mufick*, to which alone (and not to the other, the *Playne and Simple Part* :) the *Refolution* of thefe doubts may in this cafe be thought neceffary.

***

The *Definitions* and *Divisions* of *Moode Time, & Prolation* in *Measurable Musick.*

Ensurabilis *Musice* is defined to be a *Harmony* of diuers sortes of *Sounds,* exprest by certaine *Characters* or *Figures* called *Notes,* describd on *Lines* & *Spaces,* different in *Name, Essence, Forme, Quantity,* and *Quality,* which are sung by a *Measure* of *Time*; or as(1) *Io: Dunstable,* (2) the man whome *Ioan. Nucius* in his Poeticall *Musicke* (and diuers others) affirme to be the first that inuented *Composition*) saith, it hath his beginning at an *Vnite,* and increaseth vpward by two and by three infinitely, and from the highest decreaseth in like manner downe againe to an *Vnite.*

Measure in this *Science* is a *Quantity* of the *length and shortnes* of *Time,* either by *Naturall sounds* pronounced by *Voice,* or by *Artificiall,* vpon *Instruments.*

Of this *Musick, Franchinus de Coloniâ* was the first *Inuentor*; and to guide our knowledge the better, obseruing the same course that *Guido Aretinus* did, (who instituted the forme of *Plaine, or Simple Musick*) He made *Scales or Tables,* in the which all things pertaining to the diuision of *Perfect and Imperfect Measures* are contained, and by the which we may by degree attaine to the perfection of this *Knowledge.*

The *Scales or Tables* (by him instituted) of diuers are vulgarly termed *Moodes,* by some of better vnderstanding, *Measures*; and consist of *Notes, Pauses, Degrees, Signes, Perfection,* and *Imperfection.*

(1) *Io: Dunstable Mensurabilis. Musica cap I.*

(2) *Io: Nucius musica Poetica cap. I.*

B   A *Note*

Of Notes.

A *Note* is a *Signe*, or *Character* repræsenting either a *Natu-rall*, or *Artificiall Sound* : and it is two fold ;

    1. *Simple*
    2. *Compound.*

Simple Notes (Like Nowne Subſtantiues) require none other to be ioyned with them, to ſhew their ſignes, or ſignifications; of which there are 8. (1) the firſt fiue are cal'd *Eſſentiall* the laſt 3. *Collaterall*. 1. *Large*, 2. *Long*. 3. *Breue* 4. *Semibreue*. 5. *Minime*. 6. *Crotchet*. 7. *Quauer*. 8. *Semiquauer.*

(1) *Glareanus Dodecachord. lib. 3. cap. 4.*

Compound Notes (Like Nowne Adiectiues) cannot ſtand by themſelues, but require another to be ioyned with them to ſhew their ſignes and ſignifications & ariſe from the 4. firſt *ſimple Notes. Larg, Long, Breue, & Semibreue;* which being fitly *conioyn'd* one with another, we terme *Ligatures*; of which, thoſe that are with   (2) *plikes* or *ſtrokes* in *Qua-drate formes* are called *Rectes,* thoſe that are by crooked ones (3) *Obliques,* either aſcending or deſcending; in the *Charactering* of which, that at the *beginning*, that in the *Middle,* and that at the *latter end* muſt ſpe-cially be obſerued.

(2)(1) *Io: Dunſt. Muſ. cap. 12.*

For enſamples, I refer all to thoſe forraine *Authors,* that haue at large diſcourſt of the particular præcepts of this part of *Muſicke :* but domeſtically to (4) *Maſter Tho: Mor-ley* who will ſatiſſye any curious obſeruer.

(4) *Tho: Mor: lib. 1. fol. 9. 10. 11.*

Theſe *Ligatures* were inuented for two reſpects : 1. for the *Ditties ſake* 2. (without *Ditty*) for breuity of *Pricking.* But in regard the *Notes* now in vſe are not of ſo long a quantity, as when the *Perfect Moodes* were vſed, the moſt part of the *Notes Ligatur'd,* & *Ligatures* themſelues are layd aſide, except the *Breue* & *Semibreue,* which yet are retayned for the cauſes afore mentioned.

                The 4.

The 4. laſt *ſimple notes*, *Minime*, *Crotchet*, *Quauer* & *Semi-quauer* are therfore not *Ligable*, becauſe they are not *Meaſu-red*; for the(1) *Minime* is the firſt *Note* that *Meaſureth* (being in it ſelfe indiuiſible) and the *Semibreue* the firſt *note Meaſured*; and therefore the firſt *Note ligable*; And for the other 3. *Crotchet*, *Quauer*, and *Semiquauer*, they are neither aug-mented nor diminiſhed, but keepe one continuall quantitie, ^{text}

The firſt 4. *ſimple Notes* (2) *Franchinus* Inuented; & although part of their formes were not in the originall as now they are *charactered*, yet their *Meaſures* were all one : hee was al-ſo the firſt that deuided the *Large* into 3. *Longs*, and the *Long* into 3. *Breues*, and the *Breue* into 3. *Semibreues*, (further then which in thoſe dayes the *Meaſure* tended not) & all of them into 2. likewiſe; whereby he was the firſt that In-uented *Perfection*, and *Imperfection*.

The *Minime* (3) *Ph. Vitriaco* (the Flowre of *Muſitians* of all the world in his time) inuented, obſeruing the ſame forme that *Franchinus* did, deuiding the *Semibreue* into 3. *Minimes*, and into 2. at the leaſt, and term'd it *Prolation*; but as for the *Minime*, not counting otherwiſe of it then as of an *Vnite*, or a *Poynt* in *Geometry*, he reckoned it no *Time*, but the beginning of *Time*, and the very beginning of *Meaſurable Muſicke*; and ſo in theſe dayes further then the *Minime* the *Meaſure* tends not, it being the firſt and ſhorteſt *Note* that any *Meaſure* can begin on; as contrarywiſe the *Large* is the laſt and longeſt *Note*, that the voyce of man with one Breath can deliuer.

And as for our *Crotchets*, *Quauers*, & *Semiquauers*, I yet finde not the Inuention of them; and therefore I ſuppoſe no great heede was taken of the Inuentor, yet they were accepted vpon ſufferance; yet ſo, as that we now differ from the auntient in the naming of them, (4) for that which we terme our *Quauer*, they term'd a *Crotchet*, & that which

Marginal notes:
(1) *Io: Dunſt. Menſ. Muſ. cap. 16.*
(2) *Ibidem cap. 3.*
(3) *Ibidem cap 6.*
(4) *Ibidem cap. 6.*

we

vve terme a *Crotchet*, they term'd a *Semi Minime*, the halfe of our *Minime*, as the *Semibreue* is the halfe of the *Breue*. And theſe *Simple* and *Compound Notes* are they, which wee commonly call the *Inward ſignes* of *Meaſurable Muſicke*.

Of Pauſes, *or* Reſts.

PAuſes, or *Reſts* are ſilent *Characters*, or an *Artificiall* omiſſion of the voyce, repræſenting the *quantity* of the *Inward notes*, or *Signes*, as they are *Meaſured* by the *outward Signes*, which were Inuented for 3. cauſes. 1. For *Cloſes*, 2. for *Fuges*, 3. for avoyding of *Diſcords*, and diſallowances.

Examples of Inward ſignes and reſts.

Large, Longe, Breue, Semi-breue, Minime, Crotchet,

Quauer, Semi-quauer.

Of Degrees.

DEgrees were inuented to expreſſe the *value* of the aforeſaid principall *Notes*, by a *Perfect* and *Imperfect Meaſure*. *Perfect Meaſure* is when all goe by 3. *Imperfect Meaſure* when all go by 2. & *Degrees* are three-fold:

     1. *Moode*
     2. *Time*
     3. *Prolation.*

As all

(¹) As all other things haue a *Moode*(saith *Glarean*)so hath *Musicke*; and *Modus* signifieth a manner of something to be repræsented; and heere are all *Notes* of a *Square Quadrat* forme, and thereby are appropriated *Largs* and *Longs*, measured by the least of this forme, the *Breues*. (¹) *Glareanus Dodecachord. lib. 3. cap. 5.*

Tempus signifieth a Time, (²) which is ordained by order, hauing a iust *Measure*, set *Limits* & *Bonds*: and here is a figure or *Note* of a (³) *Rhombus* or *Circular* forme, which we terme the *Semi-breue*; but the reason why the *Time* is appropriated to the *Breue* is in regard of the *Perfect Measure* of the *Breue* by this *Circular Note*, though in the forme it is applyed to the *Semi-breue*. (²) *Plutarch.*

(³) *Glarean lib. 3. cap. 1. Sebald: Heyd: lib. 2. cap. 1.*

Prolation signifieth an extending or putting foorth; and it is of the *Degrees* from the first measuring *Note* to the last measured, through the *Perfect* and *Imperfect* figures; vnto which terme *Prolation* is applyed, a *Note* of a *Circular* body, but with a *Stroke*, as a head ioyned to that *Body*, which is term'd the *Minime*; (which (⁴) *Minime* measuring the *Semi-breue*) thereby comes it, that the *Tearme Prolation* is appropriated to the *Semi-breue*, as being the first *Note* measured by the *Prolationate*, or extending *Note*. (⁴) *Sebald. Heyd: lib. 2. cap. 2. Gla. lib. 3. cap. 5.*

And all three of these *Degrees*, are 2. fold, (⁵) *Maior* & *Minor*: (⁵) *Io: Dunstable Mensurabilis Musica. cap. 16.*

The *Greater Moode perfect* is, when a *Large* containes 3. *Longs.*
The *Lesse Moode perfect* is, when a *Long* containes 3. *Breues.*
The *Greater Mood Imperfect* is, when a *Larg* containes 2. *Longs.*
The *Lesse Moode Imperfect* is, when a *Long* containes 2. *Breues.*
Time perfect is, when a *Breue* containes 3. *Semi-breues.*
Time Imperfect is, when a *Breue* containes 2. *Semi-breues.*
Prolation perfect is, when a *Semi-breue* containes 3. *Minimes.*
Prolation Imperfect is, when a *Semi-breue* containes 2. *Minimes*

B 3   *Of*

Of Outward Signes.

TO thefe *Degrees* there were added certaine *Outward Signes,* the better to diftinguifh the *Perfection* and *Imperfection* of *Moode, Time,* and *Prolation.*

(¹) *Glarean Dodecachord. lib. 3. cap. 6.*
To the(¹) *Moode* expreſſing the *perfection* of it is attributed a *Ternary number* thus: 3.

(²) *Sebaldus Heydon. lib. 2. cap. 1.*
To the (²) *Imperfection* the *Binary* expreſt thus 2. (³) or the *Ternary* omitted.

Orustheparchus lib. 2. cap. 4. 5.

(³) *Morley. lib. 1. folio. 4.*
But in the firſt Age of the Inuention of this *Art,* it was expreſt by *Reſts* or *Pauſes* of their *Notes,* and in regard of the little vſe of the *Moodes,* and the *Practicall* occaſion of ſuch *Reſts* for *Cloſes,* and comming in of *Fuges,* they were layd aſide, and theſe *Numbers* aforeſaid accepted.

⁴ *Glare. Dode. lib. 3. cap. 6.*
The *Perfection* of *Time* (⁴) (as growing out of *Circular motion*) is expreſt by a *Round Circle,* thus ○.

(⁵) *Ibidem. lib. 3. cap. 8.*
The *Imperfection* of it by a *Semicircle* thus ⊂ (⁵) As for thoſe that would haue the *Number* ſignifie the *Time,* and the *Circle* the *Moode, Franchinus, Glareanus,* and diuers auncient *Theoriks* Iuſtly reprehend them.

To *Prolation,* for the expreſſing of the *perfection* thereof is atributed a *Poynt* or *prick,* ſignifying the indiuiſibility of the *Meaſure* which is placed in the midſt of the *Circle* thus ⊙ or the *Semicircle* thus ⊙ as by it preſence it cauſeth *Perfection*; ſo by the abſence thereof it cauſeth *Imperfection*; But thoſe ſlender *Artiſts,* which would haue the *Ternary number* ſignifie the *Perfect Prolation,* and the *Binary* the *Imperfect,* (and ſo onely appropriated) the aforeſaid Authors condemne, as moſt ignorant of theſe *Meaſures.*

Furthermore theſe aforeſaid *Degrees* are deuided into 4. *Tables,* by ſome term'd *Moodes,* by others 4. *Prolations,* (but wrong by both, for of *Moodes* and *Prolations* there are but 2. the *Great* & the *Leſſe*) but by the beſt vnderſtādings,

4. manner

4. manner of *Figures* are approued to diftinguifh the *Perfection* and *Imperfection* of thefe *Degrees*, by which all *Song in* this kinde is *meafured*.

Examples of the 4.Figures.

{
1 *Perfect* of the *more*
2 *Perfect* of the *Leſſe*
3 *Imperfect* of the *more*
4 *Imperfect* of the *Leſſe*.
} *Prolation.*

1 **P**Erfect of the more *Prolation* in his proper forme, is, when there is *Perfect Moode, Perfect Time,* and *Perfect Prolation,* and is thus *Charactered.*

Example.

Large								
Longs	3	Breues.	3	Semb	3	Min	3	crot 2	qua. 2	ſemiq 2
Brenes	9	Sembr.	9	Min.	9	Crot.	6	qua 4	ſemq
Semibreues	27	Min.	27	Crot.	18	qua.	12	ſeiq 8
Minimes	81	Crotch	54	Qua.	36	Seiq.	24
Crotchets	162	Qua.	.08	Semi.	72
Quauers	324	Semi.	216
Semiquauers	648

{ This Table, and the reft following expreſſe all *perfection,* and *imperfection,* and the quantity of the *Diuiſible* and *Indiuiſible Notes,* how many goeth to a *Large.*

Perfect

Before the former example this *Charatter* of the *Perfect* of the *More Prolation* should be plac'd thus. ⊙
3

PErfect *of the lesse Prolation* or the lesse extenuation in the lesse *Perfect Moode* in his proper forme (according to those, whose ensamples ought to be the same with their reasons) in my opinion should be thus *Charactered* ○. but with divers it is thus ○, thus ○, and thus ○; according to which differences, wee finde great *Maisters* in their workes (especially in their ensamples) much ranging, although the most of them confesse this (1) *Perfect of the lesse Prolation* to be the *lesse Moode Perfect: Time perfect,* and the *great Moode,* (which is 3. *Longs* to the *Large*)and *perfect Prolation* (which is 3. *Minimes* to the *Semi-breue*) to bee *Imperfect,* and that *Perfection* is by 3. and *Imperfection* by 2. Why? either the omitting of the *Numbers,* and the *Binary Number* signifying *Imperfection,* or the single *Ternary,* although in the *Perfect of the more Prolation,* the single *Ternary* noteth the *Perfection* of both *moodes,* (2) and wheresoeuer the *Greater* is there is the *Lesse,* but not contrarily; by which reason it makes good the aforesaid *Charactering,* and allowes vs for the signifying of the greater *Moode Imperfect* the *Binary Number,* for the *Lesse Moode perfect* the *Ternary,* for the *Time perfect* the *Round Circle,* and for *Prolation Imperfect,* the absence of the *Point* or *pricke; Example.* ○
2.3.

(1) *Sebal: Hey: lib.* 2. *cap.* 1. *Glarea. Dode lib.* 3 *cap.* 5. *Iohn Dunst. cap.* 10. *Ornitho: lib.* 2 *cap.* 4. *Morley lib.* 1. *fol.* 13.

(2) *Ornitho. lib.* 2. *cap.* 5.

Example

Example of the *Perfect* of the *Leße Prolation* in the
Meaſure and *diuiſion* of the *Notes*.

O
23

Large.														
Long	2	*Brues*	3	*Semib*	3	*Min.*	2	*Crot.*	2	*qua*	2	*Sem*	2
Breues	6	*Semib.*	9	*Min.*	4	*Crot.*	4	*quau.*	4	*Se.*	4		
Semibreues	18	*Min.*	18	*Crot.*	12	*quau.*	4	*semiq*	4				
Minimes	26	*Crotch*	36	*quau.*	24	*semiq* 16							
Crotchets	72	*quauer*	46	*Semi.*	48								
Quauers	144	*Semiq.*	144										
Semiquauers 288													

THeſe 2. *Perfect Moodes* in theſe dayes are of little or no
vſe, and therefore I haue little to ſay to them concerning their *Diminutions*; only I finde that the Auncients expreſt them by *Stroks* drawn through their *Circles*: In the *Per-*
fect of the More for the great *Diminution* thus, (1) ⊙ for the
Leße thus (2) ⊕ In the *Perfect of the Leße* for the great thus
(3) Ⓞ for the *Leße* (4) ⊕ but theſe for the moſt part are out of
vſe, only we finde in diuers *Church* & *Madrigall Compoſitions*,
the *Perfect of the Leße* in his great *Diminution* expreſſing *Ses-*
qui-altera Proportion thus *Charactered* (5) ⊙ ⅔ & by diuers examples for *Triple proportion* thus (6) Ⓞ ⅓. but becauſe theſe 2.
Imperfect Moodes following are now only in vſe, I will
ſomewhat ſpeake of the abſurdities committed in the *Cha-*
ractering of their *Meaſures*, eſpecially for the *Prolations* &
Diminutions; whereby wee may diſcouer what things are
neceſſarie and *Art-Like*, & reiect thoſe *Vn-Art-Like Formes*
which by Ignorance are crept in.

(1) *Glarean.*
Dode. lib. 3.
cap. 11.
(2) *Seb.alt Hey-*
don lib. 2.
cap 6.
Loſſio Se-
nior. lib. 2.
cap 6.
Morley lib. 1.
fol 25.
(3) (4) *Ibidem.*
(5) *Glarec: Do-*
de. lib. 3.
cap. 11.
(6) *Sebald.*
Heyd. lib. 2.
cap. 6.

I Mperfect of the *More Prolation* (which is the extenuation
of the *perfect prolation* through the *Imperfect Moodes* and

C 　　　　　　　　　　　　　*Time*)

Time) in the proper forme of it is, when wee haue *Imperfect Moodes, Imperfect Time,* and *Perfect prolation,* all *Notes
Measured* by 2. (ſaue the *Semi-breue* which is by 3. and by
all approued *Theorickes* thus *Character'd.* ☉

Example of the Imperfect of the
More Prolation.

Larg													
Longs	2	Breues.	2	Semb	2	Min	3	crot	2	qua.	2	ſemiq	2
Breues	4	Semibr	4	Min.	6	Crot.	6	qua	4	ſemq	4		
Semibreues	8	Min.	12	Crot.	12	qua.	12	ſeiq	8				
Minimes	24	Crotch	24	Qua.	24	Sēiq	24						
Crotchets	48	Qua.	48	Semi	48								
Quauers	96	Semi.	96										
Semiquauers	192												

BVt now *Practiſe* hath ſo infected this *Meaſure,* eſpecially
in the *Prolation* and *Diminution* of it, that when a *Perfect
Artiſt* comes to ſing a ſong of ſuch *Practicall Charactering,*
(ſuppoſing it to bee *Character'd* according to the iuſt *Perfection* and *Imperfection* of the *Degrees*) hee ſhall bee (almoſt)
as far to ſeeke for the *Meaſure* intended, as were they that
Compos'd it to ſeeke for the true *Charactering* of that *Meaſure,*
they would haue expreſt.   For that I may giue inſtance
herein, I finde it by them thus exampl'd ☉3 or thus ☉,
the which indeed I muſt confeſſe is the *Imperfect Time,* and
the *More Prolation*; But then I demannd to what end tends
that *Ternary Number?* Hereto they will anſwere (eſpecially
thoſe who in conceyt are Maſters   that it is to ſignifie a
Triple Proportion, by which the S ong before which it is ſet,
                                                      muſt

muſt be ſung; and that is (ſay they) 3. *to one.* True; but then aske them *what three to one?* and they will tell you, 3. *Minimes* to one *Semi-breue;* O moſt *Vnproportionate Cuſtomable Compoſitors,* whoſe Art ſerues them not ſo much as to diſtinguiſh *Prolation* from *Proportion!* For *Prolation* is, when 3. *Minimes* goe to one *Semi-breue,* and *Triple Proportion* is, when 3. *Semi-breues* to one *Semi-breue,* as being a *Proportion of the Greater Inæquality,* and (as wee terme it) *Multiplicis generis,* that is when a *Greater Number* is compar'd with a *Leſſer,* and containeth the *Leſſer* many Times as $\frac{3}{1}\frac{6}{3}\frac{9}{5}$ &c. It is euident then, that this ſingle *Ternary Number* cannot ſtand for a *Triple Proportion,* ſeeing it wants a *Leſſer Number* to bee compar'd with all; and beſide that, were there a *Number* adioyn'd, yet the ſigne of the *Imperfect Time,* the *Perfect Prolation,* [1] (and *Number* cannot work vpon *Prolation* ⁽¹⁾*Ornitho.* ſo long as the *Circle* retaines the *Poynt,*) the *Charactering* of *lib. 2. cap. 8.* the *Note* in white, the breaking of the *Meaſur'd Notes,* and the *Meaſure* of a *Leſſer Quantity* and *Quality* to the *Tact,* would all reſolue vs, 'tis no *Triple Proportion.*

Others then being beaten from that opinion, and yet not doubting but to hit the marke, make anſwer; Some, that the *Number* is there ſet to ſignifie, that 3. *Minimes* went to a *Semi-Breue,* in their idle conceites neuer remembring that the *Poynt* in the *Semi-Circle* ſignifies that ſufficiently: Some, that it is to ſignifie the *Moode,* not regarding that the *Meaſure* it ſelfe confutes them, in as much as this *Ternary Number* ſignifieth *Perfection,* and the *Moodes* in this *Meaſure* are *Imperfect.* And laſtly, Some (rather then faile) will haue it ſignifie *Time,* quite forgetting (as good *Authors* obſerue) that 'tis the *Circle* which ſignifies it, which being broken in this *Meaſure,* makes it therefore *Imperfect.*

May I not then wel conclude, that ſeeing this *Number* ſignifieth neither *Proportion,* nor *Prolation,* nor *Imperfect moods,*

nor

nor *Time*, 'tis but an Intruder, and by right muſt be wholy
left out in the *Meaſure* of the *Perfect Prolation?* which being
graunted, I will ſay no more of it, as making account that
it is a thing generally knowne.

The vſe of this *Perfect Frolation* is, in *Seruice Diuine* for
Iubilees and *Thankeſgiuings*, and otherwiſe for *Galliards*
in *Reuellings*.

But in this *Meaſure*, I obſerue another great *error* committed by them, which expreſſe the *Seſqui-altera-Proportion*
with 3. *White Semi-breues*, belike not vnderſtanding, that
herein *a White Semi-breue* contaynes 3. *Minimes*, if it be not
Imperfected by a *Leſſe Note* going *before*, or *following*; Yet
will they (forſooth) haue 3. of theſe *White Semi-breues* goe
to the *Tyme* of 2. *Tacts* or *Strokes*; whereas, in all nature of
Proportions, it (contrariwiſe) ought to bee expreſt with
3. *Semi-breues Denigrated*, and ſo ſignifying *Diminution*;
which then containe the *quantity* that they ayme at, of
two *Strokes* in this *Perfect Prolation*,

Example.

Error  *Truth*

VNto this *perfect Prolation*, there pertaines a 2. folde
Diminution, the *Greater* and the *Leſſer*; ſignified by *Internall*, and *Externall Signes.*

(1) *Io: Magirus
de Art. Muſicæ.*

(1)*Internall* by the *Denigrating* or blacking of the *Inward*
or *ſimple White Notes* without the *Externall Signe*,
Diminiſhe the *Tact*, as much as the *Externall Signe* it
ſelfe of the *Great Diminution* : Examples of which wee
finde

finde Diuers, in *Church Songs*, *Madrigalls*, and such like
as thus:

And diuers others there are both in the *Perfect* and *Imperfect Measures*, all pertayning to the *Great Diminution*.

The *Externall Signes* are those which are set, at the beginning of *Songs*, and are the *Characters* of the *Degrees*, for the *Diminishing* of the *White* and *Blacke Notes*, by *Dash* and *Retort*, in the *Great* and *Lesse Motion* of the *Tact*.

The *Great Diminution* and the *Externall Signe* to signifie it in *White*, is by a retort of the *Semi-Circle* with the *Character* of *Prolation* thus

Example.

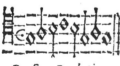

Perfect Prolation

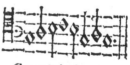

Great Diminution.

Otherwise ioyning the *Externall* and the *Internall Signes* together, 'tis thus signified,

Whereas

Whereas the cõmon practise (in *Compofition* for *Church Songs, Madrigalls, Paftoralls, Ballads,* &c.) charactereth this *Diminution* with *denigrated Notes,* and the *Outward figne* by the *Ternary Number* thus :

THey feeme to drawe their Reafons (as fome *Mafters* haue affirm'd) from the 3. fwift feete in *Poetry, Trochæus, Iambus* and *Tribrachius,* in regard of the *Notes* that are *Diminifhed.*

But then why it fhould bee apply'd more to this *Diminution* then to the *Perfect Prolation* I fee no Reafon at all; by caufe how e're the *Tact* of this *Diminution* be of a fwifter *Motion,* yet the *Meafures* are all one in the diuiding of the *Semi-breue,* according to thofe feete. As 1. *Trochæus,* which is one long and the other fhort, a *Semi-breue* and a *Minime.* 2. for *Iambus,* which by way of *Retort* to the former is one fhort and the other long, a *Minime* and a *Semi-breue.* 3. for *Tribrachius,* which is three fhort, the *Semi-breue* diuided into 3. *Minimes;* which diuifion (fay they) pertaines only to the *Diminution* and not to the *Perfect Prolation;* How beit many meane Practitioners are able to contrary that, and they who aright vnderftand *Poetry,* and *Muficke* fhall be Iudges, who knowe the *Meafure* to bee all one, and the differences of the *Motion* to bee according to each *Rule,* or according to the difcretion of them that *Sing,* or *Reade* them.

But the matter here we chiefly ftand vpon is, that the *Ternary Number* ought vtterly to be reiected, as hauing no manner of intereft either in the *Perfect Prolation,* or the *Diminutions* therof : The *Perfect Prolation* we fpake of before; and now for the *Diminution* thus I fay, that if by their *Trochaick* reafon they will bring this *Ternary Number* in, to fignifie

nifie this *Diminution*; they may as well, yea they muſt ne-
ceſſarily, to euery diuiſion of the *Semi-breue*, (which may
bee as diuers, as is the *Compoſers* Inuention) ſet a ſeuerall
Character to ſignifie it, and their applications of it to the
feete, by which it is *Meaſured*: But what a confuſion would
that be to the *Performer*, (beſides the euidence of their ridi-
culous ignorance) to charge each Diuiſion with a particular *Character*, when only the *Externall* and *Internall Signes*
ſet at the beginning of *Harmonyes* are thereto ſufficient?
And if it bee vnneceſſary to *Charactere* all, I ſee as little
reaſon that they ſhould *Charactere* any one: Or if yet they
needs'will, that one be *Charactered*, then let them ſhow
me, why the *Meaſure* of theſe other feete, which belong
to the Diuiſion of the *Imperfect Prolation* and the *Diminutti-*
ons therof, (as *Spondæus, Pyrrychius, Anapæſtus, Bacchius, Anti-*
bacchius, &c.) ſhould not aſwell be *Character'd* by them, as
theſe that belong to the diuiſion of the *Perfect Prolation,* and
the *Diminutions* of it. For if they hold *that* a thing needleſſe
and ſuperfluous to be done in a caſe ſo common and obui-
ous: the conſequence will be altogether as good againſt
this their Poeticall, phantaſticall *Charact'ring* with the *Ter-*
nary Number.

But ſee how one error begets another; It is that which I
haue obſerued as a moſt groſſe *Abſurditie* in the pricking
of the *Internall Signes* of this *Diminution,* and yet is to be
found among thoſe, whome our *Vulgar Practitioners* account approued *Maſters,* & in that opinion haue followed
their *Vn-art-like Example;* which is, the ſetting of it with a
White Minime and a *Crotchet,* and the *Tact* charactered with
the aforeſaid *Ternary Number;* as thus

Their Apologie (vpon exception taken) prooued
like

like their enſample, both fond, and ſenceleſſe; to witt,
that they might *Character* the *Sounds* in what forme it
pleaſed them, and needed not to be bound to follow the
Lawes and *Rules* of *Art*, which they found were herein wholy againſt them.

(1) Morley lib.
3. fol. 15.

THe *Leſſer Diminution*, (which is vulgarly call'd (1) *Diminution* of *Diminution*, or the *Double Diminution* of the *Perfect Prolation*) is the ſwifteſt *Motion* that any *Tune* is *Compoſed*
of vnder this *Meaſure*, as *Country Daunces, Bran'ſls, Voltos,
Courantos*, & ſuch like : And it likewiſe we find character'd,
to ſignifie the *Tact* of it, with the *Ternary Number*, which is
yet of all the reſt the greateſt *Abſurdity*: For herein there are
ſixe Notes Meaſured to one *Tact*, (whereas afore but 3.) and
Their *Ternary Number* is made to ſignifie no leſſe then *Perfect
Prolation, Great Diminution*, & *Leſſe Diminution*, and all vpon
the bare and groundleſſe warrant of *Common Practiſe*,
which ſay they, hath ſo receiu'd it, & therefore they vſe it.

But what a confuſion will this be when they haue a *Song*
or *Tune* compoſed of all theſe *Tacts*, (as diuers there are in
vſe for *Maskes* and *Reuells*) and ſhall finde but onely one
Character to expreſſe all *Motions*: how can that worke be
perform'd in his proper nature, except the *Compoſer* ſhall
either Demonſtrate by a *Canon* what his meaning is, or
himſelfe perſonally be there to explaine his *Forme* intended? Therefore the Authors of our *Art*, foreſeeing the
Diuerſities (and there by the *Abſurdityes*) which heerein
would be inuented concerning the *Diminutions* of the
Tact, agreed vpon certaine *Rules* and *Characters* together,
to Demonſtrate euery particular *Motion* by, of what kinde
of *Diuiſion* ſoeuer the *Tact* was. But now in regard that
thoſe *Canons* and *Proportionate Rules* are out of vſe, I ſee no
reaſon why wee ſhould vſe their *Characters*, but rather
be led by that *Rule*, whereof now in theſe dayes our practiſe

tife confifts , which is the *Circular Rule*, and by which this leffer *Diminution* of the *Perfect Prolation* (the *Internall Notes* being *Denigrated*) is thus *Charactered.*

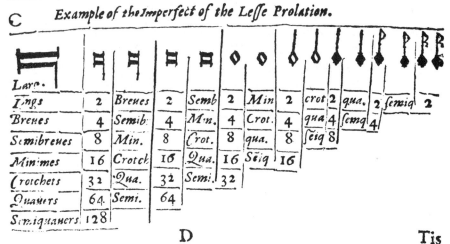

As for any motion of *Tact* fwifter then this *Leffer Diminution* if there fhould bee need thereof, it fhould be either thus *Charactered* ⊕ or by the former *Retorted* thus ꝑ Wherein the *Stroke* drawne through the *Semi-circle* and the *Prick* in it, doe fignifie a Coniunction of both *Prolations* by a *double Diminution* of the *Perfect* and *Imperfect Measures* of the *Tact.* And thus much fhall fuffife for the banifhing of the *Ternary Number,* and the placing in fteed thereof the true *Character* of the *perfect Prolation,* with the *Diminution* of it by the *Circular Rule.*

THe *Imperfect of the Leffe Prolation* ; in the proper forme of it is, when there is *Imperfection* of all *Notes Meafurable,* from the *Larg* to the *Minime*;and is thus Truely *Character'd* C and vnder it are compofed, as *Divine Services* for the Church, fo alfo *Mottets, Madrigals, Pavins,* and fuch like for other vfes.

C   Example of the Imperfect of the Leffe Prolation.

Larg.														
Lngs	2	Breues	2	Semb	2	Min	2	crot	2	qua.	2	femiq	2	
Breues	4	Semib:	4	Mn.	4	Crot.	4	qua	4	femq	4			
Semibreues	8	Min.	8	Crot.	8	qua.	8	feiq	8					
Minimes	16	Crotch	16	Qua.	16	Seiq	16							
Crotchets	32	Qua.	32	Semi.	32									
Quauers	64	Semi.	64											
Semiquauers	128													

D   Tis

NOw as before I did in the former, so in this *Measure* also haue I obſerued diuers abſurdityes committed, by not diſtinguiſhing the *Leſſe Prolation* from his *Diminutions.*

For vnto this *Time* and *Prolation* there pertaines a 2. folde *Diminution* (by[1] ſome termed *Semi-dity*) the *Greater*, and the *Leſſer.*

[1] *Glarean· Dode.lib.3. cap 10. Frederichus Berbuſius cap.12. Ornitho:lib.2 cap 8.* [2] *Sebald: Heyd. lib.2. cap.6. Freder:Berbuſius cap.12.*

The *Greater Diminution* is rightly thus *Charactered*[2] Ȼ or (by *Retort* of the aforeſayd *Imperfect Circle*) thus Ɔ; though diuers there be, that from the *Proportionate Rule* (forſooth) will haue it thus Ȼ 2. but for as much as in this *Meaſure* there is vs'd no *Denigration*, and all *Proportions* are out of vſe ſaue *Seſqui-altera*, I haue ſayd ſufficiently for confutation thereof, before.

Vnder this *Diminution* are compos'd *Almayns, Free Mens Songs, Ayres* and ſuch like, and (accordingly) among our *Minſtrells*, 'tis knowne by the name of *Almayne Time*, and is as a *Duple* to the *Leſſe Prolation*; that is, a *Motion* as ſwift againe, as the *Leſſe Prolation* is of, in his owne *Naturall Tact.*

[3] *Morley lib. 1 fol.15.* [4] *Sebald. Heyd: lib.2. cap. 6. Nicholai Liſtenij lib. 2. cap.4.*

The *Leſſe Diminution* we finde to bee thus *Character'd*[3] Ȼ, or with *Retort* of the *Great Diminution* thus[4] Đ; and this is the ſwifteſt *Motion* that vnder this *Meaſure* is Compos'd; and ſuch are all thoſe *Compoſitions* which are vnder it, as *Iiggs*, and the like.

But heerein now the Ignorance of our times is ſuch, not knowing the differences of this *Imperfect Prolation* and the *Diminutions* therof, that they commonly *Charactere* the Church *Songs*, and *Mottets*, with the *Greater Diminution* thus Ȼ; according whereunto if thoſe *Songs* ſhould be ſung, it would not only alter the nature of thoſe *Harmonies*, but alſo make them ſeeme rather ſome *Dauncing* or *Reuelling Meaſure*, then a religious *Note* tobe vſed in Gods Seruice.

'Tis then the *Leſſe Prolation* (thus Ȼ) wherewith all ſuch

Diuine

Diuine *Compositions* (especially thofe which are with *Fuges*) ought to bee *Character'd,* and that is the flowest and graueft *Meafure* now in vfe.

And fo againe for thofe *Madrigalls, Paftoralls, Pauens,* and fuch like, which are *Character'd* with this *Great Diminution,* fhould they be fung according to the *Tact* thereof, they would make fuch a confufion, that the *Performers* would furely bee taken for mad-men, and the *Songs* themfelues would feeme no better then common *Iigs* to the hearers.

Wherefore it concernes the *Compofer* to vnderftand the differences of thefe *Tacts,* and according to the nature of the *Compofition* difcreetly to *Charactere* them, that both *Himfelfe,* and his *Workes* may haue their due commendation.

And thus much breifly for the true *Charactering* of the 4. *Figures* or *Meafures,* concerning the *Perfection, Imperfection,* and *Diminutions* of *Moode, Time,* and *Prolation.* Onely thus much more of *Diminution* it felfe I muft craue leaue to adde, namely, the *Defcription* and *Vfe* of it, that it is a certaine(1)Decreafing of the *Quality* (and not of the *Quantity*) of the *Notes* and *Refts,* by *Internall* and *External Signes:* or(2)when the *Element* is abated in the Greater, or *Leffer* of the *Nature* of it; and it was inuented to haften the *Tact,* for a reuiuing of the Eare, when it is dul'd and wearied with a flow *Motion;*(3)Not that the *Number* or value of the *Notes* is thereby Diminifhed, but only that the *Tact* for the *Motion* of it is haftened, both in the *Perfect* and *mperfect Meafure.*

(1) *Glareanus. Dod: lib.* 3. *cap.* 8.

(2) *Magirus cap.* 12.

(3) *Ornithos lib.* 2. *cap.* 8.

And this by the Ancients was obferued 3. wayes.

    1 By a *Canon.*

    2 By *Proportionate Numbers.*

    3 By *Retort* of the *Semi-Circle* and a *Dafh.*

    1 Now the *Canon* being cleane out of vfe, we haue nothing at this time to fpeake thereof : and the like alfo for

Proportionate Numbers; in regard common practise hath disused all proportions saue *Sesqui-altera* we haue little to say of them.

As for the *Ternary* and *Binary Numbers* which should be brought in by way of this *Proportionate Diminuti-on*, expressed by *Glareanus* with these examples (as from the common practise in those dayes) C, C, 3 C C 3 and thus with a *Ternary Number* alone 3; He and diuers other auncient *Theorists* affirme (in regard of the *Diminutions* of the *Degrees*) that they are nothing but fancies of the ignorant *Vulgar Practitioners*; for saith he (speaking of the *Diminution* of the *Degrees*, and ther-by of the *Circular Rule*) what needs there to expresse the *Diminutions* of the *Degrees*, any more, then onely the *Retort* and the *Dash*, and so reiect all the rest, that the common *Cantors* should not be confounded in these rules, him-selfe and diuers others giuing these examples ☉. ⊕. C. ⊕. C. Ɔ. C D or thus C. C. Ɔ or thus C. D or thus C: to which as very resonable and onely necessary, for the practise of these *Times* (all others being contrary) I subscribe.

(·) Glarean. Dod: lib.3. cap. 11.

Of Tact.

---

(1) Sebald: Heyd. lib. 2. cap. 5.
(2) Morley lib 1 fol 9. Nicholis Li-stenij. cap. 10.

Tact, Touch or *Time*, is, a certaine (2) *Motion* of the hand (whereby the quantity of *Notes* and *Rests* are di-rected) by an equall *Measure*, according to the properties of the *Signes* of the *Degrees*. The Auncients obserued three

    1 The *Greater*.
    2 The *Lesse*,
    3 The *Proportionate*.

                                   But

But thefe our dayes obferue but two, and thofe deriued from the former obferuations.

The firft is the *Perfect Diuifion* of the *Semi-breue* which is by 3. the which we call *Minime Time*, & as fome fay, from the *Proportionate Rule*.

The fecond is the *Imperfect Diuifion* of the *Semi-breue* which is by 2. the which we terme the *Semi-breue Time*, and as fome fay, from the *Diminifhed Breue*.

All which *Tact* or *Time* according to the difcretion of the *Singer* (and according to the *Meafure*) may be fung fwifter, or flower.

BEfides all thefe, vnto thefe foure forefaid *Figures* or *Meafures*, there appertaine diuers other *Rules*; As *Augmentation, Sincopation, Imperfection*, the *Pricks* of *Perfection, Addition, Diuifion, Alteration*, & fuch like; All which ferue to diftinguifh the *Diuifion, Alteration*, and *Augmentation* of *Perfect* and *Imperfect Notes*; but becaufe we haue little or no vfe of the moft of them, faue the *Pricke* of *Addition*, ((2)which fome terme that of *Perfection*, others of *Augmentation*, making little difference betweene them) at this time I'le fpeake of it onely, and not of the reft.

A *Prick* is a *Signe* of an *indiuifible Quantity* placed either before, after, on the vpper, nether ends, or fides of a *Note*, and there feruing for the aforefaid diftinctions.

This *Pricke* of *Addition* placed on the right fide of a *Note*, (thus) in *Perfect Time*, & *Perfect Prolation* if a *Minime* or a *Leffe* *Note* follow, caufeth the fame to be *Perfect*; and in *Imperfect Time* it maketh the faid *Note*, if a *Breue* or *Semi-breue*, to be *Perfect*, but as for *Leffe Notes*, being *Indiuifible*, it doth *Augment* thefame to be halfe fo long againe, as the *Quantity* of it affoorded.

And

(1) Mor'ey *A-nota*. fol. 5.

ANd laſt of all, as neceſſary to all *Harmonies*, pertaine
certaine *Signes* for diuers vſes, as *Repetitions*, thus *Charact'red.* ‖: ÿ :)(: ?.

Conueniences thus

Concordances, or *Cardinalls* thus as *Pauſes*

Connexions, when two *Notes* are ioyn'd together both
for the better ordering of *Diſcords*, and the applying of
the *Note* to the *Ditty* thus ; all which this worke
is full of.

Index or *Director* thus

And theſe *Signes*, let me entreate all thoſe which would
performe theſe *Harmonies* in their proper Nature, ſtrictly
to obſerue; which if they will doe, with the *Diſtinctions* of
the *Prolations* and *Diminutions*, they ſhall doe the Authors
much right, and no doubt giue themſelues & the hearers
good contentment.

This then is it I had now to ſay concerning the neceſſary
Rules of this part of our *Art*, as pertaining to the vſe of our
Common Practiſe. If my *Labours* herein proue as *Accep-
table* as they are *True* and *Neceſſary*, it will giue me
much incouragement to proceed further in a generall *Suruey* by me intended ; if not, I ſhall
perhaps become loath to beſtow my
Talent in ſuch a *Fruitleſſe*
Soile.

F J N J S.

Errata in the Harmonies.

3. for *Peirce* read *Peirs*.

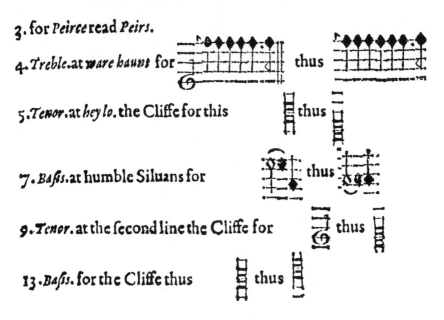

4. *Treble.* at *ware haunt* for ———— thus

5. *Tenor.* at *hey lo.* the Cliffe for this ———— thus

7. *Bass.* at humble Siluans for ———— thus

9. *Tenor.* at the second line the Cliffe for ———— thus

13. *Bass.* for the Cliffe thus ———— thus

Errata in the Discourse.

In diuers of the bookes, in the *Rule* of the *Perfect* of the *Lesse* his *Character* is thus, folio 8. ☉ ☉ ☉ ☉, but should be thus ☉ ☉ ☉ ☉

folio 13. in the fourth *Example* of *Internall Signes*.

for ———— thus ————

folio 17. for Direction 'Tis, read Now.
folio. 20. line 7. for the *Characters* of the *Imperfect* of the *Lesse* ℂ C.3. thus C3 C2.

Hunting,
&
Hawking,

A *Hunts* vp.

Tenor.　　　IOHN BENNET.　　　4. *Voc.*

THe *hunt* is vp, :||: ſing merrily wee,

the *hunt* is vp, ſing merrily wee, the *hunt*

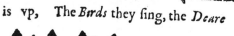

is vp, The *Birds* they ſing, the *Deare*

they fling, hey nony nony nony no, the *Hounds* they crye, the *Hunters* they flye,

hey tro li lo, tro lo li lo, hey tro lo li lo li li lo.　　　The *hunt* is vp, *vt ſupra.*

The *Woods* reſounds
To heere the *Hounds*,
　hey, nony nony-no:
2　The *Rocks* report
This merry ſport,
　hey, trolilo trololilo.
Cho. { The *hunt* is vp, the *hunt* is vp,
　　　　Sing merrily wee the *hunt* is vp.

Then hye apace
Vnto the *chaſe*
　hey nony, nony nony-no
3　Whilſt euery thing
Doth ſweetly ſing,
　hey troli-lo trololy-lo.
The *hunt* is vp, the *hunt* is vp,
Sing merrily wee the *hunt* is vp.

A *Hunts* vp.

Iohn Bennet.

MEDIVS.   4. VOC·

Cho:

He *hunt* is vp, the *hunt* is vp, fing merrily wee the *hunt* is vp, fing

verfe

merrily wee the *hunt* is vp.   *Hey downe*

Cho:

The *Hunt* is vp, *vt fupra.*

TREBLE.   4. VOC.

Cho:

He *Hunt* is vp, the *Hunt* is vp, fing merrily wee, the *Hunt* is vp,

verfe

fing merrily wee, the *Hunt* is vp: *hey downe*

Cho

the *Hunt,* &c.

BASIS.   4. VOC.

Cho:

He *Hunt* is vp, the *Hunt* is vp, fing merrily wee, the *Hunt* is vp,

verfe

fing merrily wee, the *Hunt* is vp.   *Hey downe*

Cho

The *Hunt* is vp, *vt fupra.*

For *Hunting*.

EDVVARD PIERS.

TREBLE.   4. *VOC.*

Ey trola, trola, hey trola, trola, there,

there boyes there :||: hoicka, hoick, :|': whoope :||:

Crie there they goe, crie, there they goe, they goe, they are at a fault,

Boy winde the Hor ne, Ho rne, *Boy*, winde the Ho rne,

TENOR.   4. *VOC.*

Ey trola, trola, hey trola, trola, there, there boyes

there, :||: boyes there: hoicka hoick, whoop: :||: crye

there they goe, crye there they goe, they goe, they goe, they are at a fault:

Boy winde the Ho rne Ho rne *Boy*, winde the Ho rne.

EDVVARD PEIRS.

MEDIVS. 4.VOC

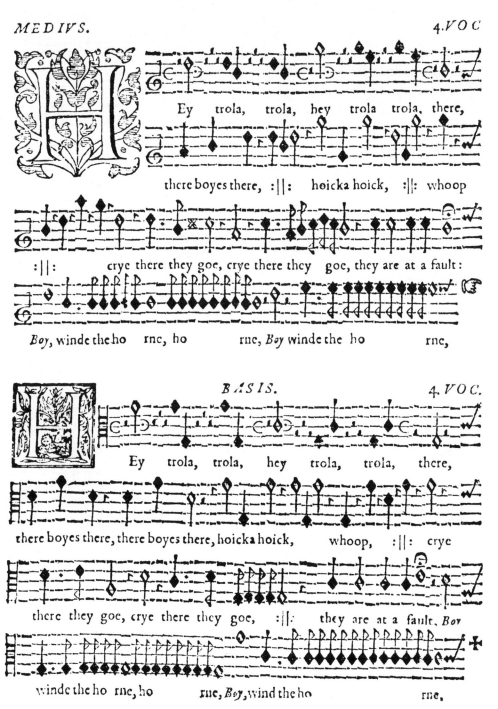

Ey trola, trola, hey trola trola, there,

there boyes there, :||: hoicka hoick, :||: whoop

:||: crye there they goe, crye there they goe, they are at a fault:

Boy, winde the ho rne, ho rne, Boy winde the ho rne,

BASIS. 4.VOC.

Ey trola, trola, hey trola, trola, there,

there boyes there, there boyes there, hoicka hoick, whoop, :||: crye

there they goe, crye there they goe, :||: they are at a fault, Boy

winde the ho rne, ho rne, Boy, wind the ho rne.

The *Hunting* of the *Hare*.

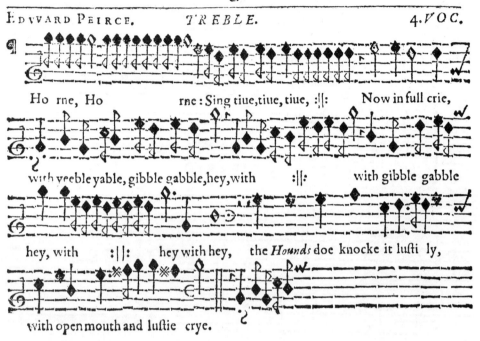

Ho rne, Ho   rne: Sing tiue, tiue, tiue, :||:   Now in full crie,

with yeeble yable, gibble gabble, hey, with :||: with gibble gabble

hey, with :||: hey with hey, the *Hounds* doe knocke it lufti ly,

with open mouth and luftie crye.

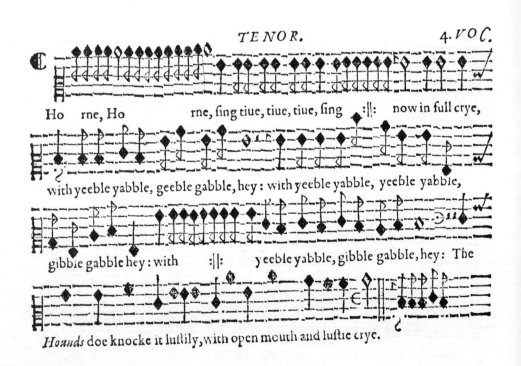

Ho rne, Ho   rne, fing tiue, tiue, tiue, fing :||: now in full crye,

with yeeble yabble, geeble gabble, hey: with yeeble yabble, yeeble yabble,

gibble gabble hey: with :||: yeeble yabble, gibble gabble, hey: The

Hounds doe knocke it luftily, with open mouth and luftie crye.

The Hunting of the Hare.

Edvvard Peirce. MEDIVS. 4.VOC.

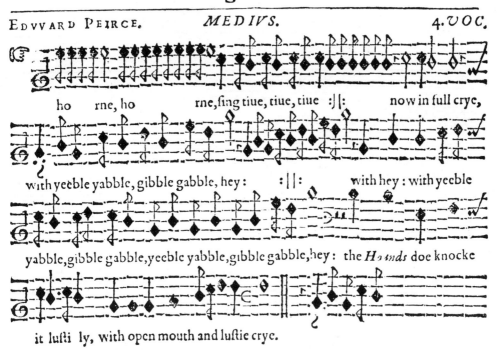

ho   rne, ho   rne, sing tiue, tiue, tiue :||:   now in full crye,

with yeeble yabble, gibble gabble, hey :   :||:   with hey : with yeeble

yabble, gibble gabble, yeeble yabble, gibble gabble, hey : the Hounds doe knocke

it lusti ly, with open mouth and lustie crye.

BASIS.   4.VOC.

Ho   rne, Ho   rne, sing tiue, tiue, tiue : sing   now in full crye,

with yeeble yable, gibble gabble hey, with :   :||:   with yeeble yable,

gibble gabble, yeeble yabble, gibble gabble, hey : The Hounds doe knocke

it lustily, with open mouth and lustie crye.

A *Hawkes*-vp, for a *Hunts* vp.

THOMAS RAVENSCROFT. Bachelar of *Muſicke*.

MEDIVS.

4. VOC.

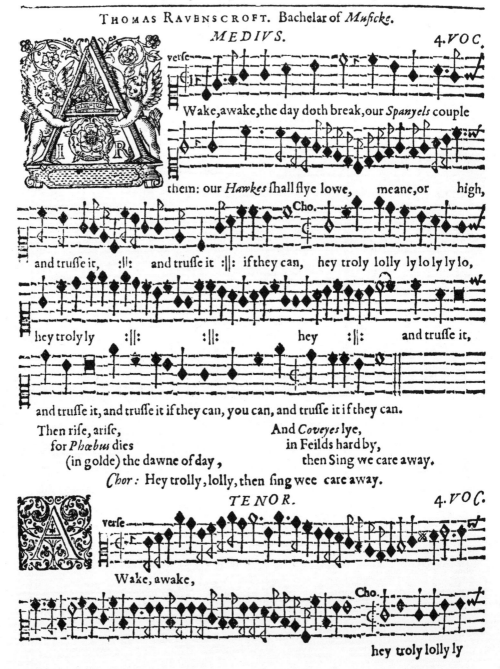

verſe

Wake, awake, the day doth break, our *Spanyels* couple

them: our *Hawkes* ſhall flye lowe, meane, or high,

and truſſe it, :||: and truſſe it :||: if they can, hey troly lolly ly lo ly ly lo,

hey troly ly :||: :||: hey :||: and truſſe it,

and truſſe it, and truſſe it if they can, you can, and truſſe it if they can.

Then riſe, ariſe,
  for *Phœbus* dies
    (in golde) the dawne of day ,

And *Coveyes* lye,
  in Feilds hard by,
    then Sing we care away.

Chor: Hey trolly, lolly, then ſing wee care away.

TENOR.

4. VOC.

verſe

Wake, awake,

Cho.

hey troly lolly ly

TENOR.   4.*VOC*

lolly lo hey,   :||:   :||:   :||:   hey troly loly lo, and truffe it,

and truffe it, and truffe it if you can you can, and truffe it if you can.

TREBLE.   4.*VOC.*

Wake   Cho

hey troly lo

ly ly lo ly ly lo hey   :||:   hey   hey ||:

and truffe it,   :||:   and truffe it if you can you can, and truffe it if you can.

BASIS   4.*VOC*

wake,
Cho

hey troly lo ly lo ly lo, hey troly lo ly lo   :||:   hey tro lo ly

lo and truffe it, and truffe it, and truffe it if you can, and truffe it if you can.

B

MEDIVS.   Tʜᴏᴍᴀs Rᴀᴠᴇɴsᴄʀᴏꜰᴛ.   Bach: of *Muſicke.*   4. *VOC*

Ith *Sickles* & the ſheering *Sythe,* hath ſhorne the Feilds

of late, now ſhall our *Hawkes* & we be blythe, Dame *Partridge*

ware your pate: our murdring *Kites,* in all their *flights,* wil ſild or neuer neuer neuer

ſeld or neuer miſſe, To truſſe you euer euer euer euer, & make your bale our bliſſe,

whur ret *Duty,* whur ret *Beauty* ret, whur ret *Loue,* whur ret, hey dogs hey :||:

TENOR.   4. *VOC.*

Ith Sickles

whur ret *Cater,* ret *Trea,*

TREBLE.   THOMAS RAVENSCROFT. Bach. of *Musicke.*   **4. *VOC.***

Ith Sickles

whur ret,

whur ret, *Quando* ret, whur ret, *Nimble* ret, hey dogs hey :||: dogs hey,

BASIS.   **4. *VOC.***

Iith Sickles

whur ret, whur ret, *Trauell* ret, whur ret, *Trouer* ret, hey dogs hey   :||:

whur ret *Iew*, whur ret, *Damsell* ret, whur ret, hey dogs hey, hey dogs hey,

MEDIVS.

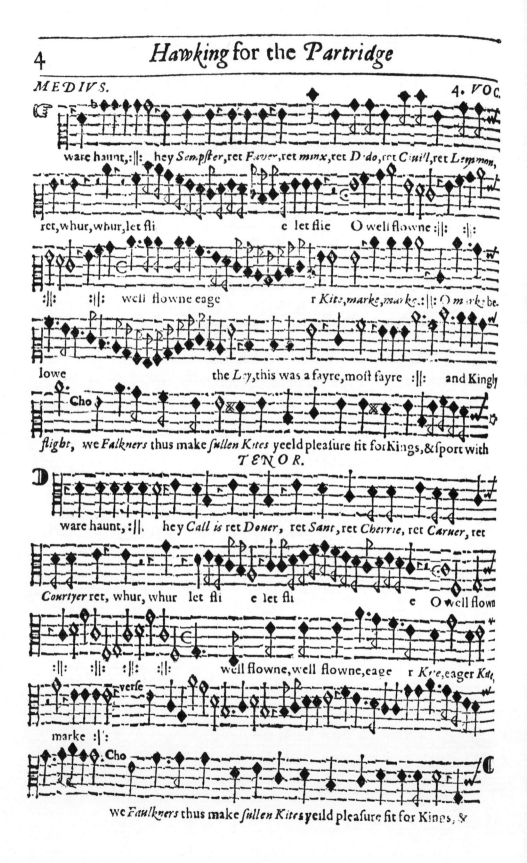

ware haunt, :||: hey *Sempster*, ret *Faver*, ret *minx*, ret *Dido*, ret *Ciuill*, ret *Lemmon*,

ret, whur, whur, let fli   e let flie   O well flowne :||:   :||:

:||:   :||:   well flowne eage   r *Kite, marke, marke.* :||: *O marke* be.

lowe   the *Ley*, this was a fayre, most fayre :||:   and Kingly

Cho

flight, we *Falkners* thus make *sullen Kites* yeeld pleasure fit for Kings, & sport with

TENOR.

ware haunt, :||:   hey *Call is* ret *Dover*, ret *Sant*, ret *Cherrie*, ret *Caruer*, ret

Courtyer ret, whur, whur let fli   e let fli   e   O well flown

:||:   :||:   :||:   :||:   well flowne, well flowne, eage   r *Kite*, eager *Kite*,

verse

marke :||:

Cho

we *Faulkners* thus make *sullen Kites* yeild pleasure fit for Kings, &

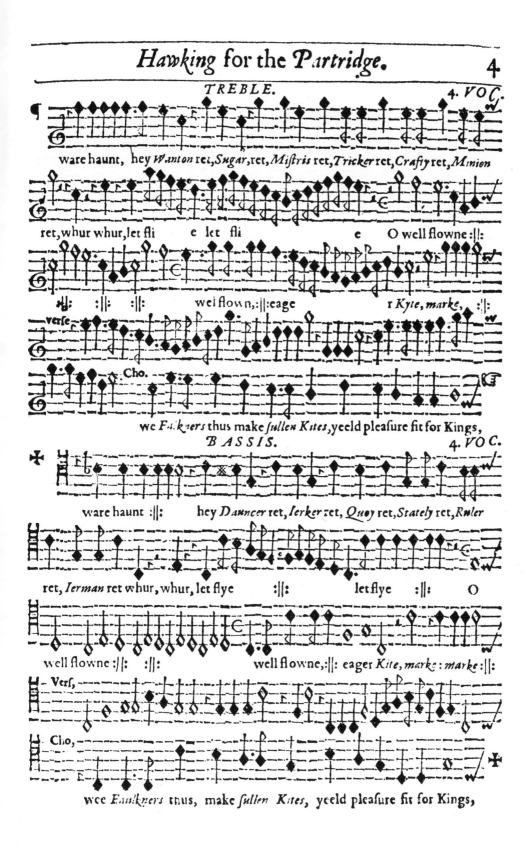

TREBLE.   4. *VOC.*

ware haunt,   hey *Wanton* ret, *Sugar*, ret, *Miſtris* ret, *Tricker* ret, *Craſty* ret, *Minion*

ret, whur whur, let fli   e let fli   e   O well flowne :||:

:||:   :||:   :||:   wei flown, :||: eage   r *Kyte*, marke,   :||:

verſe

Cho.

we *Falkners* thus make *ſullen Kites*, yeeld pleaſure fit for Kings,

BASSIS.   4. *VOC.*

ware haunt :||:   hey *Dauncer* ret, *Ierker* ret, *Quoy* ret, *Stately* ret, *Ruler*

ret, *Ierman* ret whur, whur, let flye   :||:   let flye   :||:   O

well flowne :||:   :||:   well flowne, :||: eager *Kite*, marke : marke :||:

Verſ,

Cho,

wee *Faulkners* thus, make *ſullen Kites*, yeeld pleaſure fit for Kings,

MEDIVS.   4 VOC.

them :|||:   and :|||:   in thofe delights, and oft, and oft

in other things, and oft :|||:   in other things.

TENOR.

fport with them, and :||:   :|||:   with them in thofe delights, & oft in

other things, and oft   :|||:   oft in other things.

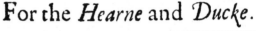

5   For the *Hearne* and *Ducke*.

TREBLE.   IOHN BENNET.   4. VOC

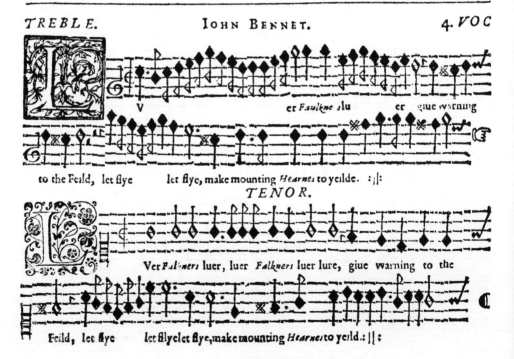

V

er *Faulkne* slu   er giue warning

to the Feild, let flye   let flye, make mounting *Hearnes* to yeilde. :||:

TENOR.

Ver *Falkners* luer, luer *Falkners* luer lure, giue warning to the

Feild, let flye   let flyelet flye, make mounting *Hearnes* to yeild.: ||:

THOMAS RAVENSCROFT. Bach. of *Muficke.*
TREBLE.

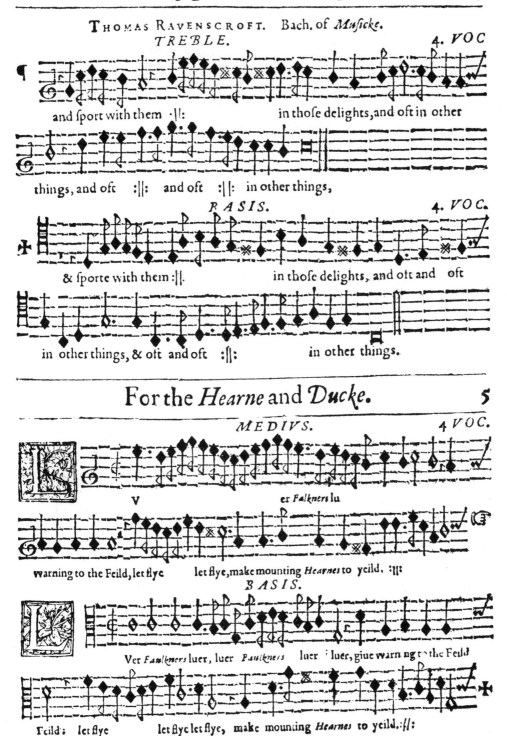

and fport with them ·||: in thofe delights, and oft in other

things, and oft :|||: and oft :|||: in other things,

BASIS.

& fporte with them :|||. in thofe delights, and oft and oft

in other things, & oft and oft :|||: in other things.

For the *Hearne* and *Ducke.* 5

MEDIVS. 4 *VOC.*

er *Falkners* lu

warning to the Feild, let flye let flye, make mounting *Hearnes* to yeild. :|||:

BASIS.

Ver *Faulkners* luer, luer *Faulkners* luer luer, giue warning to the Feild

Feild: let flye let flye let flye, make mounting *Hearnes* to yeild.:|||:

TREBLE.   4. *VOE.*

Dye fearfull *Duckes*, and climbe no more fo high, :||: :||: The *Nyas*

Hauke will kiffe the Azure Skie. But when our *Soare Haukes* flye, & ftiffe windes blowe : then

long to late we *Faulkners* crye hey io, hey lo, hey lo . :||:

hey lo, hey lo . But when &c.

TENOR.   4. *VOC.*

Dye fearfull *Duckes* :||: and climbe no more fo high, and :||: The *Nyas Hauke* will

kiffe the Azure Skie, But when our *Soare Haukes* flye and fwift windes blowe, then long to late

we *Folkners* crye hey ho heylo, :||: hey lo :||: hey :||:

hey lo :||: heylo But when &c..

MEDIVS.   4.*VOC.*

Dye fearfull *Duckes* & climbe no more fo high, no :||: & :|||: The *Nyafe Hauke* will kiffe the Azure Skye, But when our Soare *Haukes* flye and ftiffe windes blowe, then long to late we *Faulkners* crye, bey lo bey lo :||: bey lo :|||: bey lo :||: bey lo :|||: lo But when our Soare &c.

BASIS.   4.*VOC*

Dye fearefull *Duckes*, and climbe no more fo high :||: no more fo high fo high. The *Nyafe Hauke* will kiffe the Azure Skye, But when our Soare *Haukes* flye, & ftiffe windes blowe, then long to late we *Faulkners* crye, bey lo bey lo :|||: bey lo :||: bey lo :|||: hey lo But when cur

TREBLE.   THOMAS RAVENSCROFT. Bach. of *Musicke*.   4. *VOC.*

Are you haunt our *hallowed greene*, none but *Fayries* heere

are seene, downe and sleepe, wake and weepe: pinch him

blacke, and pinch him *blew*, that seekes to steale a louer true. When you come to

hear vs *sing*, or to tread our *Fayrie ring*, pinch him *blacke* & pinch him *blew*, (O

TENOR.   4. *VOC.*

Are you haunt our *hallowed greene*, none but *Fayries* here are seene:

Downe and sleepe, wake and weepe, pinch him *blacke*, and pinch

him *blew*, that seekes to steale a Louer true : when you come to heare vs *sing*,

or to treade our *Fayrie ring*, pinch him *blacke* and pinch him *blew*, O

THOMAS RAVENSCROFT. Bach. of *Musicke*.

MEDIVS.   4. *VOC*

Are you haunt our *hallowed greene*, none but *Fayries* here are

scene: Downe and sleepe, wake and weepe, pinch him *blacke* and pinch him

blew, that seekes to steale a Louer true. When you come to heare vs *sing*,

or to tread our *Fayrie ring*, pinch him *blacke* and pinch him *blew*, O

BASIS.   4. *VOC*.

Are you haunt our *hallowed greene*, none but *Fayries* here are

scene, Downe and sleepe, wake and weepe, pinch him *blacke* and pinch him

blew, that seekes to steale a Louer true. When yee come to heare vs *sing*,

or to tread our *Fayrie ring*, pinch him *blacke* and pinch him *blew*, O

TREBLE.   4. *VOC*

thus our nayles shall handle you, thus our nayles shall handle you.

TENOR.   4. *VOC*

thus our nayles shall handle you, thus our nayles shall handle you.

7   The *Satyres* Daunce.

TREBLE.   THOMAS RAVENSCROFT Bach: of *Musicke.*   4. *VOC*

Ound a round a round a :||: keep your ring to the glorious

Sunne, we sing *Hoe! hoe!* he that weares the flaming *rayes,* and the Imperiall Crowne

of *Bayes,* him with him, with him, with shoutes and songs we praise, we praise,

TENOR.   4. *VOC.*

Ound a round a round a :||: keep your ring to the glorious

Sunne we sing *Hoe! hoe!* he that weares the flaming *rayes,* and the Imperiall Crowne

of *Bayes,* him with him, with him, with shoutes and songs, we praise, we praise,

MEDIVS. 4 *VOC*

thus our nayles fhall handle you, thus our nayles fhall handfe you.

BASIS. 4. *VOC.*

thus our nayles fhall handle you, thus our nayles fhall handle you.

The *Satyres* Daunce. 7

MEDIVS. 4. *VOC*

Ound a round a round a :‖: keepe your ring, to the glorious

Sunne we fing. *Hoe!, hoe!* he that weares the flaming *rayes,* & the Imperiall Crowne

of *Bayes,* him with him, with him, with fhoutes and fongs, we praife, we praife,

BASIS. 4. *VOC*

Ound a round a round a, :‖: keep your ring to the glorious

Sunne we fing. *Hoe! hoe!* he that weares the flaming *rayes,* & the Imperiall Crowne

of *Bayes,* him with him, with him, with fhoutes and fongs, we praife, we praife,

TREBLE.   4. *VOC*

hoe! hoe! that in his bountie would vouchſafe, to grace the humble, humble,

humble *Sylvans* & their ſhag   gy race.

TENOR.   4. *VOC*

hoe! hoe! that in his bounty would vouchſafe, to grace the humble,

humble, humble *Sylvanes* and their ſhaggy race.

TREBLE.   4 *VOC*

Y the moone :||: we ſport & play, with the night begins our day,

as we friske :||: :||: the dew doth fall, trip it, :||: little *Urchins* all,

TENOR.   4. *VOC*

Y the Moone, :||: we ſport & play, with the night begins our day, as we

friske, :||: :||: the dew doth fall, trip it, :||: little *Urchins* all,

MEDIVS. 4.VOC.

hoe! hoe! that in his bountie would vouchsafe, to grace the humble, humble,

humble *Syluanes* and their shag gy race.

BASIS. 4.VOC

ho! ho! that in his bounty would vouchsafe, to grace the humble, humble,

humble *Syluanes* and their shaggy race.

The *Vrchins* Daunce 8

MEDIVS. 4.VOC.

Y the *Moone* :||: we sport & play, with the night begins our day,

as we friske :||: the dew doth fall, trip it :||: :||: little *Vrchins* all,

BASSIS. 4.VOC.

Y the Moone :||: we sporte and play, with the night begins our day, as we

friske :||: :||: the dew doth fall, trip it :||: little *Vrchins* all,

TREBLE.   4. *VOC*

lightly   :||:   as the little, little bee, two by two,   :||:   and

three by three, :||:   :||:   and about goe wee, :||:   and about, about

about, about, and about, about goe we, and about, about goe we.

TENOR.   4. *VOC*

lightly,   :||:   :||:   as the little, little Bee, two by two, and three by

three, :||:   :||:   and about goe we, :||:   and about, about,

about, about, and about, about goe we, and about, about goe we.

MEDIVS.   4. *VOC.*

lightly,   :||:   as the little little *Bee*, two by two and three by three,

:||:   and about goe we,   :|.   and about about about about & about

about goe we, and about about goe we.

BASIS.   4. *VOC.*

lightly   :||:   as the little little *Bee*, two by two :||: and three by three,

:||:   :||:   :||:   And about goe we,   :||:   and about about about about

and about about goe we, and about about goe we.   '5'

D

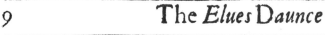

TREBLE.   IOHN BENNET.   4. *VOC.*

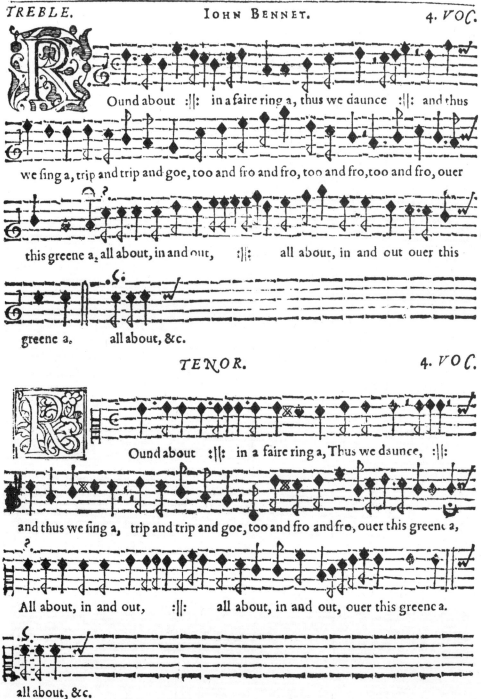

Ound about :||: in a faire ring a, thus we daunce :||: and thus

we sing a, trip and trip and goe, too and fro and fro, too and fro, too and fro, ouer

this greene a, all about, in and out, :||: all about, in and out ouer this

greene a.   all about, &c.

TENOR.   4. *VOC.*

Ound about :||: in a faire ring a, Thus we daunce, :||:

and thus we sing a, trip and trip and goe, too and fro and fro, ouer this greene a,

All about, in and out, :||: all about, in and out, ouer this greene a.

all about, &c.

MEDIVS.   4 *VOC*

Ound about: ||:   in a faire ring a, Thus we daunce,   :||:

and thus we sing a. trip and trip and goe, too and fro and fro, too and fro and fro,

over this greene a, All about, in and out,   :||:   all about in and out, ouer

this greene a,   all about, &c.

BASIS.   4. *VOC*

Ound about   :||:   in a faire ring a, Thus we daunce,   :||:

and thus we sing a, Trip and trip and goe, too and fro and fro, too and fro & fro, &

fro ouer this green a, All about, in and out   :||:   all about in and out, ouer

this greene a,   all about, &c.

Drinking.

TREBLE. THOMAS RAVENSCROFT. Bach: of *Musick*. 4. *VOC*

Rudge away quickly & fill the black Bole, deuoutly as long as wee bide,

now welcome good fellowes, both strangers and all, let madnes & mirth set sadnes

aside. Of all reckonings I loue good cheere, with honest folkes in company : and

when drinke comes my part for to beare, for still me thinks one tooth is drye.

2
Loue is a paftime for a King,
if one be feene in Phifnomie :
But I loue well this pot to wring,
for ftill me thinkes one tooth is drie.

3
Mafters this is all my defire,
I would no drinke fhould paffe vs by:
Let vs now fing and mend the fier,
for ftill me thinkes one tooth is drie.

TENOR. 4 *VOC.*

Rudge away quickly & fill the black Bole, devoutly as long as we bide,

now welcome good fellowes both ftrangers & all, let madnes & mirth fet fadnes

afide.

for ftill me thinks one tooth is drye.

MEDIVS.

4. *VO*

Rudge away quickly and fill the black Bole, deuoutly as long as we

bide, now welcome good fellows both strangers and all, let madnes and mirth set

verf

sadnes aside.

for still me thinks one looth is drye.

4 Mr. *Butler* giue vs a taste,
   of your best drinke so gently:
  A Iugge or twaine, and make no waste,
   for still me thinkes one tooth is drie.

5 Mr. *Butler* of this take part,
   ye loue good drinke as well as I :
  And drinke to mee with all your hart,
   for still mee thinks one tooth is drie.

Cho: Trudge away quickly, &c.
    now welcome good fellowes, &c.

BASIS

4. *VOC.*

Rudge away quickly and fill the blacke Bole, deuoutly as long as

we bide, now welcome good fellowes both strangers and all, let madnes & mirth

verse

set sadnes aside.

for still mee thinkes one tooth is drie.

TREBLE.   THOMAS RAVENSCROFT. Bach. of *Musicke.*   4. *VOC*

Osse the pot tosse the pot, let vs be merry, and drinke

till our cheeks be as red as a Cherry.   We take no thought

we haue no care, for still we spend, and neuer spare, till of all money our pursse is

bare, we e uer tosse the pot.

Chorus { Tosse the pot, tosse the pot, let vs be merry,
And drink till our cheeks be as red as a Chery

2 We drinke Carouse with hart most free,
    A harty draught I drinke to thee :
    Then fill the pot againe to me,
      and euer tosse the pot,   *Cho:* Tosse the pot &c.
3 And when our mony is all spent,
    Then sell our goods, and spend our rent,
    Or drinke it vp with one consent,
      and euer tosse the pot.   *Cho:* Tosse the pot &c.

TENOR.   Cho: 4. *VOC.*

Osse the pot tosse the pot let vs be merry, & drink till our cheekes

be as red as a Cherry.

MEDIVS.　　　　　　　　　　　　　　　　　　　　**4. VOC**

Offe the pot toffe the pot let vs be merry, & drink till our cheekes

be as red as a Cherry.

Cho: Toffe the pot, &c.

4　When all is gone we haue no more,
　　Then let vs fet it on the fcore,
　　Or chalke it vp behinde the dore,
　　　　and euer toffe the pot.　　*Cho:* Toffe the pot, &c.

5　And when our credit is all loft,
　　Then may we goe and kiffe the poft,
　　And eat Browne bread in fteed of roft,
　　　　and euer toffe the pot.　　*Cho.* Toffe the pot, &c.

6　Let vs conclude as we began,
　　And toffe the pot from man to man,
　　And drinke as much now as we can,
　　　　and euer toffe the pot.

Cho: ⎰ Toffe the pot toffe the pot let vs be merry,
　　　 ⎱ And drinke till our cheekes be as red as a Cherry.

BASIS.　　　　　　　　　　　　　　　　　　　**4. VOC.**

Offe the pot toffe the pot, let vs be merry, and drinke till our

cheekes be as red as a Cherry.

Of Drinking

Ale and Tobacco.

THO: RAVENSCROFT,
Bach. of Musicke.

TREBLE. 4.VOC

Obacco fumes away all naftie rheumes, but health away it neuer

lightly frets, And nappy nappy Ale makes mirth, makes mirth (as Aprill raine

doth Earth) Spring like the pleafant fpring, where ere it foaking wets.

Chorus. But in that fpring, &c.

One cleares the braine, the other glads the hart,
  which they retaine, by nature and by art:
The firft by nature cleares, by Arte makes giddy will,
  the laft by nature cheare s, by Art makes heady ftill.

Chorus. So we whofe braines, &c.

TENOR. 4.VOC

Obacco fumes &c.

Ale and *Tobacco*.

THO: RAVENSCROFT.
Bach. of *Musicke*.

MEDIVS.   4. *VOC.*

Obacca fumes &c.

Chorus. { So we whofe Braines els lowe, fwells high with Crotchet rules,
feede on thefe two as fat, as heddy giddy fooles.

BASIS.   4. *VOC.*

Obacco fumes, &c.

E

TREBLE.   4 VOC.

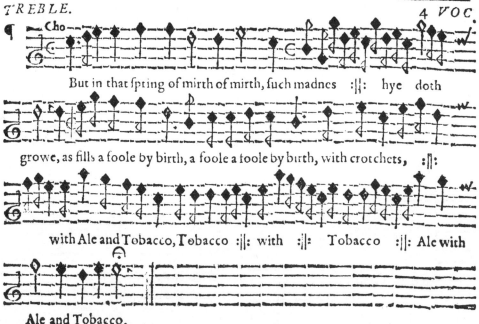

But in that spring of mirth of mirth, such madnes :||: hye doth

growe, as fills a foole by birth, a foole a foole by birth, with crotchets, :||:

with Ale and Tobacco, Tobacco :||: with :||: Tobacco :||: Ale with

Ale and Tobacco.

Chorus { So we, whose Braynes els lowe swell hye with crotchet rules,
        { Feed on these two, as fat as headdy giddy fooles.

Chorus.   *TENOR.*   4. VOC.

But in that spring of mirth of mirth, such madnes madnes, :|:| hye doth

growe as filles a foole by birth, a foole a foole by birth, with crotchets, with :||:

:||: with Ale and Tobacco, and Tobacco :||: with Ale and Tobacco, Tobacco

:||: with Ale with Ale, & Tobacco.

MEDIVS.   4. *VOC.*

But in that spring of mirth of mirth, such madnes madnes :||: hye doth

growe, as filles a foole by birth a foole a foole by birth, with crotchets :||:

with Ale and Tobacco, Tobacco, Tobacco, with Ale and Tobacco, Tobacco,

Tobacco, with Ale with Ale and Tobacco.

BASIS.   4. *VOC.*

But in that spring of mirth of mirth such madnes madnes :||: hye doth

growe, as filles a foole by birth by birth with crotchets crotchets, :||: Ale and

Tobacco, Tobacco, :||: with Ale and Tobacco, Tobacco, Tobacco, with

Ale and Tobacco.

E 2

Enamoring.

TREBLE.   IOHN BENNET.   4.*VOC*

Hat seekes thou foole, what seeks thou foole in this place?

thou foole,

thou foole,   gay cloaths and a purse of gould, foole foole, foole foole, whom a

womanfetsto schoole, foole foole, t‖: whom a woman fets to schoole, whom &c.

TENOR.   4.*VOC.*

Hat seeks,   thou foole,

thou foole   the bable of a foole, what feeks thou foole,

what feeks thou foole in this place.   foole foole :‖: whom a womā fets to schoole,

foole foole, foole foole, whom a woman fets to schoole, whom a woman fets to schoole.

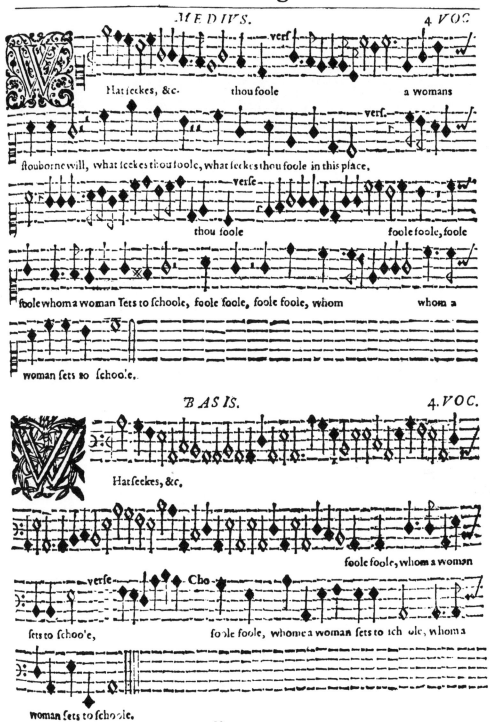

MEDIVS. 4 VOC

Hat feekes, &c. thou foole a womans

stouborne will, what feekes thou foole, what feekes thou foole in this place.

thou foole foole foole, foole

foole whom a woman fets to schoole, foole foole, foole foole, whom whom a

woman fets to schoole.

BASIS. 4. VOC.

Hat feekes, &c.

foole foole, whom a woman

verfe Cho-

fets to schoo'e, foole foole, whome a woman fets to ich ole, whom a

woman fets to schoole.

The Seruant *of his* Miſtris.

MEDIVS.   4 *VOC*

IOHN BENNET.

Y Miſtres is as faire as fine, milk-white fingers, Cherry

noſe, like twinckling day-ſtarres lookes her eyne, lightning

all thinges where ſhe goes, Faire as *Phœbe* though not ſo fickle : ſmooth as glaſſe

though not ſo brickle.

My heart is like a Ball of Snowe,
   melting at her luke-warme ſight :
Her fiery Lips like Night-worms glowe
   ſhining cleere as Candle-light.
     Neat ſhe is, no Feather lighter:
     Bright ſhe is, no Dazie whiter

The Seruant *of his* Miſtris.

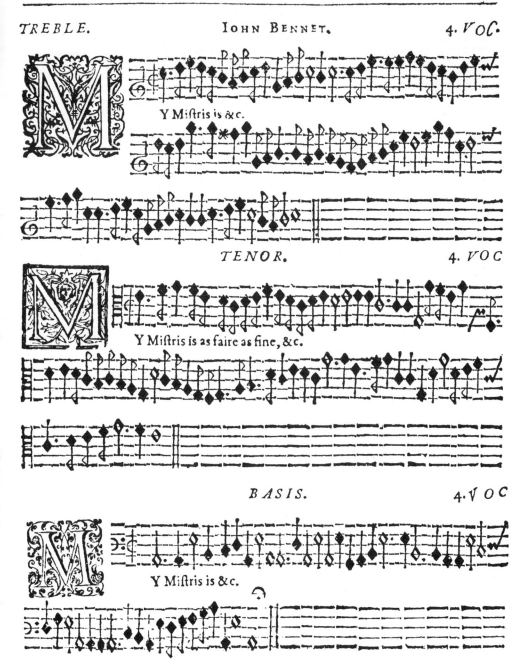

TREBLE. IOHN BENNET. 4. *VOC.*

Y Miſtris is &c.

TENOR. 4. *VOC*

Y Miſtris is as faire as fine, &c.

BASIS. 4. *VOC*

Y Miſtris is &c.

EDW: PEIRS.

TREBLE.   4. VOC

Oue for such a cherry lip, would be glad to pawne his

Arrowes, *Venus* heere to take a sip, would sell her *Doues* and teeme of *Sparrowes*,

but shee shall not so, hey no no ny no ny no, none but I this lip must owe, hey

nony nony nony, hey, :||:   hey :||:   nony no.

Did *Ioue* see this wanton eye,
   Gan:med should wayte no longer:
Phebe heere one night to lye,
   would change her face, and looke much yonger.
     but shee shall not see,
     hey no ny, no ny no.
     none but I this lip must owe,
     hey no ny, no ny no.

TENOR.   4. VOC.

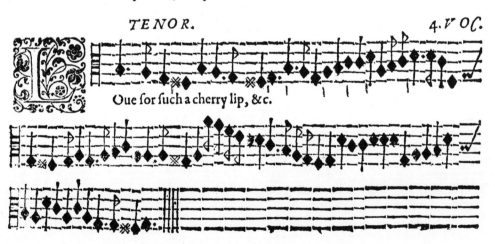

Oue for such a cherry lip, &c.

The *Mistris* of her *Seruant*.

EDW: PEIRS.

MEDIVS.   4 VOC

Oue for such a chery lip, &c.

BASIS.   4. VOC

Oue for such a chery lip, &c.

F

TREBLE.   THOMAS RAVENSCROFT. Bach: of *Musicke*.   4. *VOC*.

Eaue of *Hymen*, and let vs borrow to bid the *Sunne* good

morrow, good morrow :||: good morrow.   See the *Sunne* cannot refraine,

but doth rise and giue againe, that which you of *Hymen* borrow, and with

smiling bidst good morrow, good morrow to the *Sunne*, and to our Brides

good-night to your sweet Beauties, sweet Beauties touch your side.

MEDIVS.   4 *VOC*

Eaue of *Hymen* and let vs Borrow to bid the *Sunne* good

morrow to :||: morrow good morrow :||: good morrow.

TENOR. 4. VOC

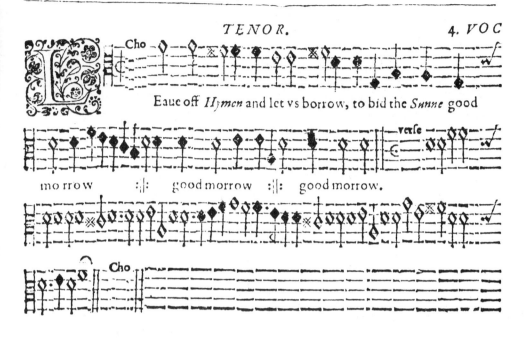

Eaue off *Hymen* and let vs borrow, to bid the *Sunne* good

mo rrow :|: good morrow :|: good morrow.

Cho

BASIS. 4. VOC

Eaue off *Hymen* and let vs borrow, to bid the *Sunne* good

Morrow, good Morrow, good Morrow, good Morrow.

Cho

Hodge Trillindle to his *Zweet* hort *Malkyn.*

Vurst bart.   D E N O R.   4. *VOC.*

Oame *Malkyn,* hurle thine oyz at *Hodge Trillindle,*

And zet a zide thy *Diſtaue* thy *Diſtaue* and thy *Zpindle,*

a little little tyny let a ma braſt my minde, to thee which I haue vownd as

ghurſt as ghinde, yet loaue ma (Zweet, Zweet, Zweet,) a little tyny vit, and

wee a little little Wedelocke wooll gommit, a little little tyny Wedelocke

wooll gommit, y vaith wooll wee, wooll wee, that wee wooll y vaith lo.

Zegund bart vollowes.

Vurſt bart   D R E B L E.   4. *VOC.*

Oame *Malkyn,* &c.

Hodge Trillindle to his Zweet hort Malkyn.

Vurſt bart.   DREBLE.   4 VOC

Zegurd bart vollowes.

Vurſt bart.   MEDVZ.   4. VOC.

Oame Malkyn, &c.

Zegund bart vollowes.

Vurſt bart.   BAZIS.   4. VOC.

Oame Malkyn, &c.

Zegund bart vollowes.

DRELE.   Thomas Ravenscroft Bach. of *Muficke.*   4. VOC.
Zecund bart.

O tell yo tell ma zo : but *Roger* I cha vound your words

but wynde : thon not for vorty bound, wooll I beeleaue yo vurther thon

Ich zee your words and deeds loyke *Beeans* and *Bacoan* gree : But if yol

loaue ma long a little little vit, Thon wedlocke Ich a little :||: wool gómit,

A little little tyny wedlocke wool gommit y vayth wooll I, thot ich

Dthurd bart vollowes.

wooll :||: thot ich wooll I vayth lo.

Zecund bart.   *MEDVZ.*   4. V OC.

O tell yo tell ma zo, &c.

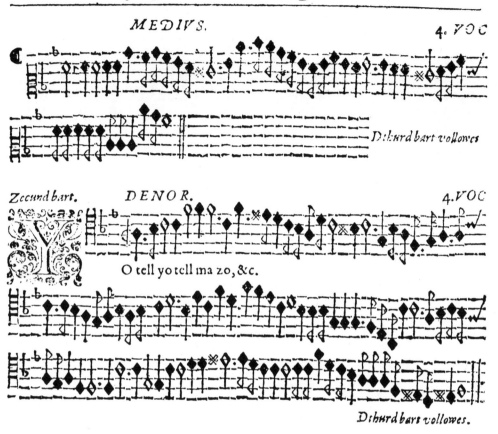

MEDIVS. 4. VOC

D:hurd bart vollowes

Zecund bart. DENOR. 4. VOC

O tell yo tell ma zo, &c.

Dthurd bart vollowes.

Zecund bart. BAZIS. 4. VOC.

O tell yo tell ma zo, &c.

Dthurd bart vollowes.

Their Goncluzion.

Malkyn.   *DREBLE.*   4 *VOC.*

Ch con but zweare, &c.   Thon *Roger* zweare

yo wooll be virmer thon yo weare : zo *Roger* zweare an oape   hold *Hodge*

O hold, oie to wyd yo gape, O hold, O hold, thow't byte I zweare my wozen.

verse   Ich do good *Hodge* thon zweare no more, Ich

wooll bee thoyne and God a bee vore, Ich :||: be thoyne, & God a beevore.

MEDVZ.   4. *VOC.*

Ch con but zweare, &c.

Cho.

Their Gonciuzion.

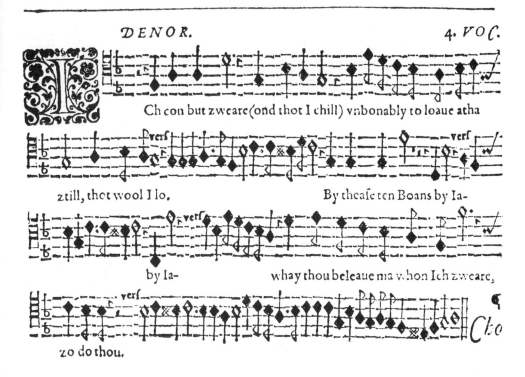

DENOR.   4. *VOC.*

Ch con but zweare (ond thot I chill) vnbonably to loaue atha

ztill, thot wool I lo.   By theafe ten Boans by Ia-

by Ia-   whay thou beleaue ma whon Ich zweare,

zo do thou.

BAZIS.   4. *VOC.*

Ch con &c.

G

The Goncluzion.

Dbuvd bars.

DREBLE.   4. *VOC.*

Thon geat wee *Growdes* ond *Boagbipes* ond :||:   ond *Boagbipes,*

Harbes ond *Dabors* :||:   to leead vs on to eand ower loaues

to eand ower loaues great labors, toeand ower loaues great labors

MEDVZ.   4. *VOC.*

Thon geat wee *Growds* ond *Boagbipes, Boagbipes* ond :||:

ond *Boagbipes, Harbs* ond *Dabors* :||:   to leead vs on to eand ower

loaues, to eand ower loaues great labors to :||:

The Goncluzion.

DENOR. 4 *VOC*

Thon geat wee *Growds* ond *Boagbipes* ond *Boagbipes* :||: ond *Boagbipes*

Harbs and *Dabors* :||: to lcead vs on to eand ower loaues, to eand

ower loaues great labors.

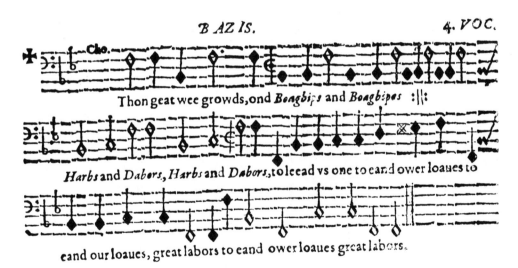

BAZIS. 4. *VOC.*

Thon geat wee growds, ond *Boagbips* and *Boagbipes* :||:

Harbs and *Dabors*, *Harbs* and *Dabors*, to lcead vs one to eand ower loaues to

eand our loaues, great labors to eand ower loaues great labors.

G 2

IOHN BENNET.

Borgens a borgens, che hard long a goe bee

verſe

merry merry :||: ond a vig vor woe,

O tis faliant ſport, then let this Burden zweet ly

zung be ztill, A Borgens a Borgen bee't good be it ill, A

DENOR.

4. *VOC.*

Borgens a borgen, cha hord long a goe, be merry merry :||: ond

verſe

a vig vor woe

MEDVZ. 4 VOC.

Borgens a Borgen cha hord long agoe be merry merry

verse

:||: ond a vig vor woe   Zing gleare zing zweet and zure, ower Zong zhall

verse

bee but zhort *Muzicke* foice, ond daunzing

BAZIS. 4. VOC.

Borgens a Borgen, cha hord long agoe, bee merry merry   :||:

verf

and a vig vor woe,

DREBLE.   4. *VOC*

A Borgens a Borgen, vor weale or vor woe.   So euer led dis blea-

fing Borden goe, So :||:   bleafing Burden goe.

DENOR.   4. *VOC.*

Borgens a borgen vor weale or vor woe, zo euer led dis bleafing borden

goe, focuer let fo :||:   fo euepled dis bleafing burdon goe.

FINIS.

Their *Wedlocke*.

MEDVZ. 4.*VOC.*

Borgens a Borgen vor weale or vor woe, zo euer led dis blea sing burden

goe, so euer led :||: dis blea sing burdon goe.

BAZIS 4 *VOC*

Borgens a Borgen vor weale or vor woe, so euer led dis bleasing burdon

goe, so euer led, so euer led dis bleasing bordon goe.

FINIS.

A TABLE OF ALL THE
Harmonies Contained in this
Booke.

FINIS.